The Abbotts

A Devonshire immigrant family in Canada

—GAIL FERGUSON—

 FriesenPress

Suite 300 - 990 Fort St
Victoria, BC, v8v 3K2
Canada

www.friesenpress.com

Copyright © 2019 by Gail Ferguson
First Edition — 2019

All rights reserved.

No part of this publication may be reproduced in any form, or by any means, electronic or mechanical, including photocopying, recording, or any information browsing, storage, or retrieval system, without permission in writing from FriesenPress.

ISBN
978-1-5255-5135-2 (Hardcover)
978-1-5255-5136-9 (Paperback)
978-1-5255-5137-6 (eBook)

1. REFERENCE, GENEALOGY & HERALDRY

Distributed to the trade by The Ingram Book Company

Table of Contents

Foreword... vii

Introduction... xi

Acknowledgements... xiii

Chapter 1: The Abbott-Kingwell Reunion............................ 1

Chapter 2: In Devonshire... 13

Chapter 3: The Immigrants... 58

Chapter 4: The Forerunners.. 82

Chapter 5: Albert Abbott (1855-1929)............................... 86

Chapter 6: William Abbott Jr. (1856-1887).......................... 90

Chapter 7: Philip Abbott (1858-1934)................................ 96

Chapter 8: Edwin Abbott (1860-1927)............................... 114

Chapter 9: Priscilla Rowse Abbott (1861-1935).................... 119

Chapter 10: John (Jack) Rowse Abbott (1863-1944)............... 125

Chapter 11: Thomas Lethbridge Abbott (1867-1925).............. 130

Chapter 12: Charles (Charlie) Henry Abbott (1869-1950)........ 135

Chapter 13: Alfred (Fred) Abbott (1873-1943)..................... 139

Chapter 14: The Abbott Legacy...................................... 144

Endnotes.. 149

Bibliography... 155

Index.. 157

PATRONIZED BY H.R.H. THE DUKE OF EDINBURGH.

LIGHT AND TRUTH

J. HAWKE
8 George Street
PLYMOUTH

NEGATIVES KEPT. COPIES CAN ALWAYS BE HAD.
THIS OR ANY OTHER PORTRAIT ENLARGED UP TO LIFE SIZE
AND PAINTED IN OIL OR WATER COLOR

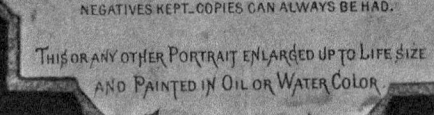

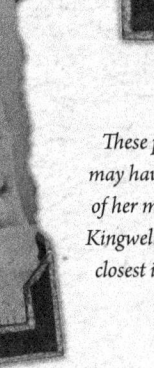

These photos are from the collection of Priscilla Abbott Baldwin. They may have been given to her by her father, William Abbott, after the death of her mother, Lydia, in 1872. None are identified, except for one "Nellie Kingwell, for Priscilla". I believe them to be images of the people who were closest in the hearts of the Abbotts as they left their home in Devon for a new life in Canada. They belong in this book.

For Callum and Archer, the next generation… with love, Grandma.

Foreword

What a read! Let us go back in time: let's say back to the 1850s, plus or minus a few years, when Canada was trying its level best to attract immigrants to its shores. Settlement in Ontario was lucrative: jobs were plentiful and wages were good.

In June of 1871 a large family from Devonshire embarked on a small steamship from Liverpool, England. They were headed for their new home in Canada. It took ten long days to cross the North Atlantic. Finally, the ship docked in Quebec City. They made their way to Southwestern Ontario. Their future lay before them. This is their remarkable story.

Gail Ferguson has been researching the genealogy of the Abbotts for more than 20 years. She writes a clear story of the Abbotts and other associated families in her ancestral line. Gail has provided the picturesque details of the Abbott homeland in South Devon. She follows the family to North Dorchester Township, Middlesex County, Ontario, tracing the family members as they struggled to settle in a new country. She then follows the descendants of the immigrant family, producing an engaging story from the facts that she has gathered. She has also left room for future research with the unanswered questions posed by the book.

The 100th Abbott Kingwell Reunion is the starting point. Oh yes! Many of us were very much a part of this annual gathering as two families celebrated their kinship for 100 years, and a great 100 years it was.

Read on and don't forget, the stories and images are all yours to enjoy!

Dr Charles Baldwin
Tillsonburg, Ontario

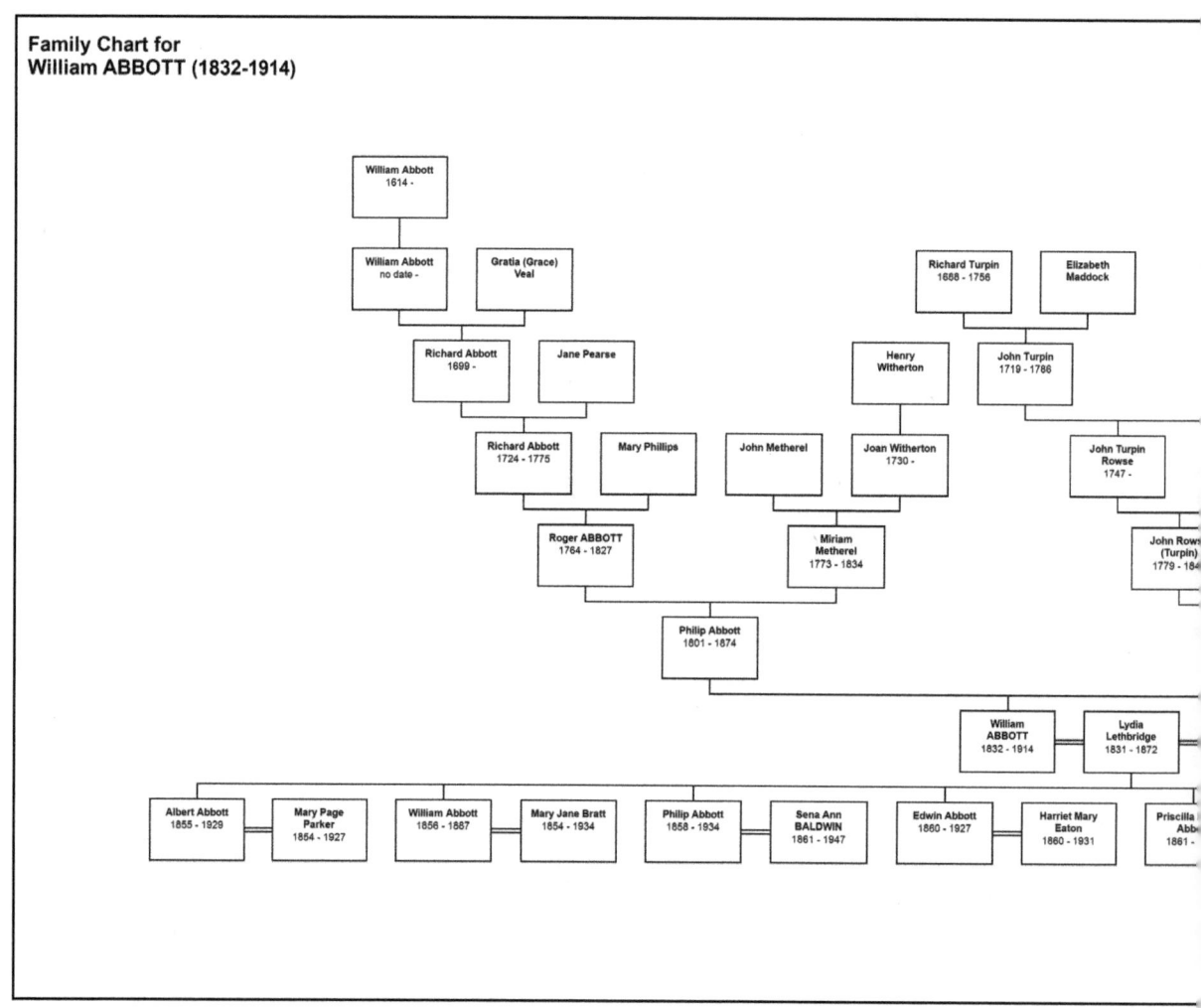

x

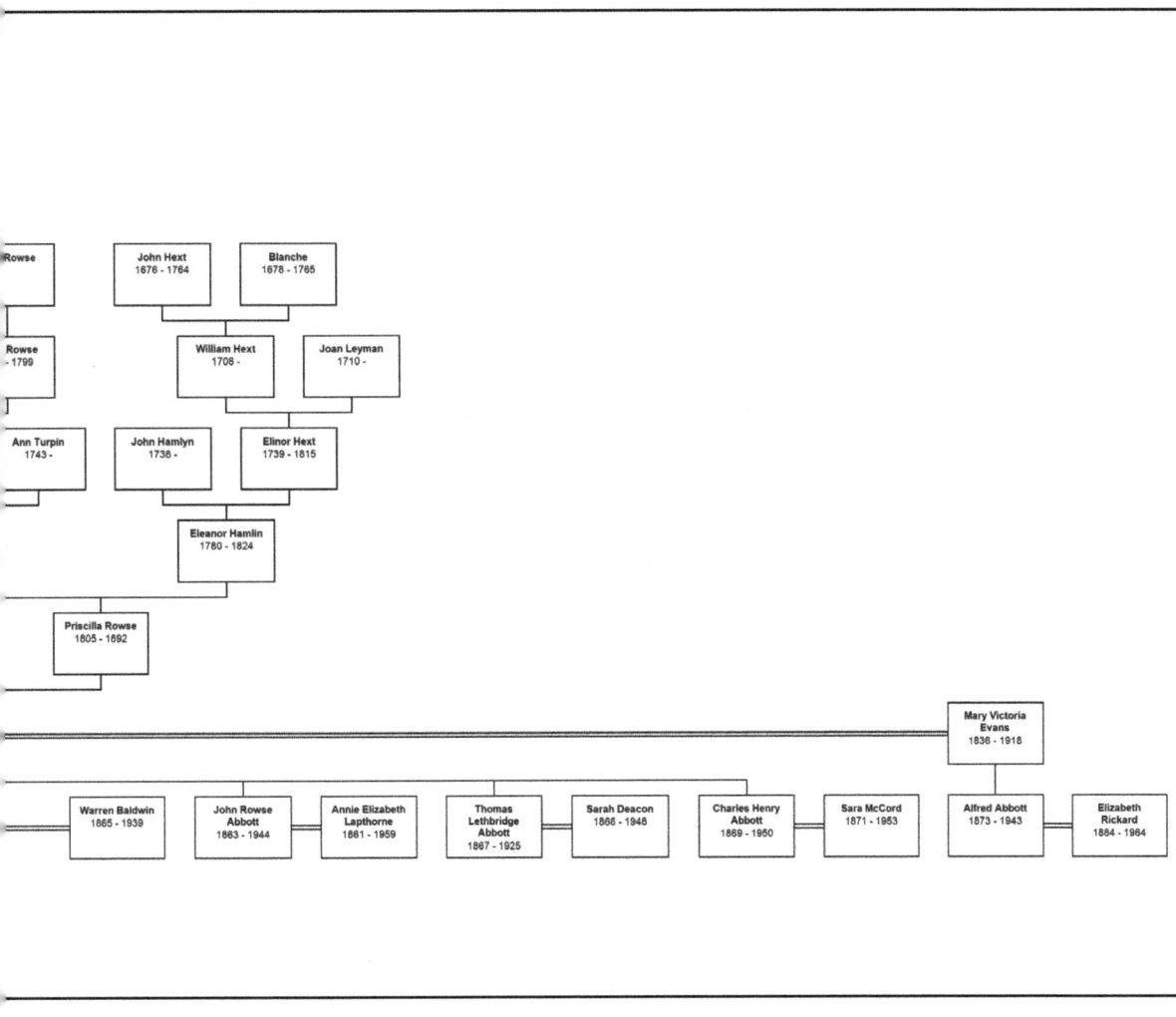

Introduction

The Abbotts: a Devonshire immigrant family in Canada is the history of the family of William Abbott (1832-1914). It is based on genealogical research, family stories, written submissions by family members, interviews, photographs, local and international travel, family trees and charts, family histories, and records of the Abbott-Kingwell Reunion. Chapters on some of the branches of William Abbott's descendant tree are longer and more detailed than others because there was more information available to me. As generations pass, information is lost, connections fade and cousins become unknown to each other. Some branches of the family had few descendants and other lines have died out completely. Many descendants shared colourful stories, detailed written narratives, and treasured family photographs, while others were not able to provide much information at all.

I did not grow up in Abbott country in either Devon, England, Southwestern Ontario or rural Manitoba. Many of my cousins are much better known to each other than they are to me. The locales in the following chapters will be as familiar to them as their own backyards. However, I hope that those, like me, who are unfamiliar with the Abbott's dwellings and environs, will find a sense of place in this family history. The references found in county directories, historical atlases, census records, maps, etc. can help to place the family in a particular time and place, framing its story.

The first chapter of this family history explores the history of the Abbott-Kingwell Reunion from the minute books that were entrusted to me in 2010. I hope they will eventually find their place in an archival repository where they can be conserved and made accessible.

Chapter two examines the Abbotts and related families in Devon, England. Here I made much use of Bernard Kingwell's family history of the Abbott and Kingwell families and added information from my own research. Chapter three examines the family of William Abbott and his first wife Lydia and second wife Mary as they immigrated and settled in Ontario. The fourth chapter examines extended family members who left Devon to become immigrants in Ontario before William Abbott. There follow chapters five through thirteen on each of the branches of the Abbott family descended from William and it is here that there is considerable variance in the amount of information and detail that was available to me. Some contain only a few pages, others are robust with detail, especially those describing very large families. The last chapter attempts to understand the legacy of William Abbott in Canada.

Acknowledgements

The Abbott Family history has been recorded by many family members. I would like to thank the following people for their willingness to share their reminiscences, research and recordkeeping and photographs with me:

- Bernard Kingwell wrote a booklet entitled, *Abbott Family Tree: Devon England to First Generation born in Canada* in 1985. His focus was the connection between the Abbott and Kingwell families. He visited descendants of William Abbott's brother Philip Abbott in Lee Mill Bridge, Devon. Bernard's work was carried out long before the automation of many of the genealogical records we use currently. I am grateful for his extensive genealogical research.
- Mary E. Abbott, daughter of Charles Abbott wrote *The Abbott Family* in 1965. Mary compiled lists of family descendants as well as an introductory paragraph about William arriving in Canada.
- Ruby Moody, for her lifelong work on the Abbott and Baldwin ancestors and descendants.
- Sena Ann (Baldwin) Abbott who composed *Mrs Abbott's Book* in February of 1941 in which she lists Births, Marriages and selected Deaths as well as several addresses.
- Several Abbott descendants in Manitoba contributed to a local history book called *Tiger Hills to the Assiniboine,* which was published by Treherne Area History Committee in 1976. Grace Abbott Vennard, Alma Abbott Henry and Lulu Abbott Harland, who made family history contributions to this publication.

- Joyce Harland and Don Bowles, who sent stories to me about their mothers Alma and Lulu and their descendants in western Canada.

- Vera Parsons, a local historian, who wrote an ongoing column in the Avon/Springfield area for many years, was a wealth of knowledge about the Abbott and Shackleton families. Her daughters Verna Stratton and Myrna Hough created a database based on Mary Abbott's work.

- Dr. Charles (Charlie) Baldwin for his work on the Abbott Reunion in recent years and his willingness to share photographs and family knowledge with me. I would also like to thank Charlie for writing the Foreword to this book and for providing advice on this project at different stages.

- Janice Brain, the wife of Howard Brain, a descendant of William Abbott Jr., who maintains a database on the Abbott family and has undertaken detailed research on the family.

- Kevin Shackleton who maintains an extensive family history database on all branches of his family including the Abbotts. Kevin has been a great source of encouragement on this book project. Having travelled to Lee Mill Bridge and other parts of South Devon to visit the Abbott's Devon heartland he has acted as a helpful sounding board during the writing of this book.

- Marlyn Brady for her narrative on the descendants of William and Mary Victoria Abbott.

- Eula Hunt, Leta Lawson, Loreen VanKoughnett, Margaret Dunn, Jean Houghton, and Janet Shackleton for stories, photographs and other details.

- Anne O'Reilly and the North Dorchester Heritage Book Committee for helping me with some of the photographs and photo credits used in the book.

- My late cousin, Wayne Shackleton, whose lively stories about the Abbotts initially got my attention. I think he would be pleased with this book.

- Maureen Selley, Secretary - Devon Family History Society for her expertise with Devon marriage and baptismal records.

- Gord Ripley for his expertise, patience and guidance during the indexing of this book

- From my own public library network, I appreciate the training and assistance I have received over the years from the staff of both the Canadiana Department, North York Central Library and the Toronto Reference Library. This publication would not have been possible without the years of experience they shared with me in research methods, collection awareness and genealogical reference inquiry. I learned much from them when I worked as a genealogical librarian and, following my retirement, as I continued my research. I would especially like to thank my friend, and former colleague, David Bain, for perusing and commenting on this work. David has lent a fresh eye to the editorial process.

There will be some that I have overlooked and I apologize for this and for any omissions and errors. The few blank pages inside the covers of this book provide space for corrections the reader may wish to make.

Finally, and most sincerely, I would also like to extend my appreciation to my husband, Joseph Romain, for his faith in this project and for his encouragement, support, judgement and technical abilities during the writing of this book. Joseph has followed my, often vague and conflicting, navigations along the road, and has walked through many a soggy cemetery with me, in Canada and abroad, in the search for elusive ancestors. Thank you, Joseph.

Chapter 1
The Abbott-Kingwell Reunion

The history of the Abbott Family first piqued my curiosity at the old schoolhouse in Avon, Ontario in 1978. I was twenty-five years old, recently graduated as a history major with no immediate job prospects. One weekend in early June, my mother prepared to head down Highway 401 from Toronto to attend the Abbott-Kingwell Reunion at the Shackleton Auction Barn near Springfield, Ontario. I had nothing else planned, so I joined her on that trip that became a long and winding journey into my family's past.

My mother, Hazel Shackleton Ferguson, loved to go to the annual family "picnic". She had grown up on a farm near Harrietsville, Ontario, but had lived in Toronto since she married in 1932. She didn't often get a chance to see her relatives. I remembered Shackleton family reunions vividly from my childhood, but the Abbott reunion was less easily brought to mind.

It was just after the buffet lunch of cold chicken and jellied salad that my ancestor-hunting cousin, Wayne Shackleton, cornered me and asked me if I knew who had started this reunion. He told the heartbreaking story of a family newly emigrated from Devon, who during their first winter in Southwestern Ontario lost the heart and soul of their family, a mother of eight children, who slipped away during childbirth. He was fascinated by their history and I soon caught the bug.

By the time I began attending the Abbott "picnic" with my own family in 1994 we were gathered at Thorndale, Ontario in the Community Centre and my children would look around and wonder how they were connected to the others assembled there. They knew no one but were charmed by a distant cousin, Leta Lawson, who paid them quarters to play tunes on a piano that was desperately in need of tuning.

My family has always indulged my interest in the Abbott-Kingwell Reunion, although they don't share my curiosity about the Abbott family. There are just too many generations separating them.

Unfortunately, I have found nothing to document the first time the Abbotts got together for a large family picnic. However, one of John (Jack) Rowse Abbott's descendants, Loreen Vankoughnett, sent me an invitation to the *Third Annual Abbott Picnic* that had been preserved by her family. The picnic was held at the London Hunt Club Grounds in Dorchester on Monday, May 26th, 1913 at noon. John Abbott was the President and Lorin (Lorne) Shackleton was the Secretary. In those days the reunion was a chance to get together with brothers, sisters and cousins who lived in various communities surrounding London, Ontario. We can assume that the first annual Abbott Picnic was held in 1911.

> The pleasure of your company is requested at
> The Third Annual Abbott Picnic
> to be held at the
> London Hunt Club Grounds, Dorchester
> Monday, May Twenty-Sixth,
> nineteen hundred and thirteen.
> Lunch Baskets opened at Twelve o'clock, noon.
>
> **John Abbott,** President.   **Lorin Shackleton,** Secretary.

Invitation to the Third Annual Abbott Picnic, 1913. Courtesy of Loreen VanKoughnett and Margaret Dunn.

Abbott Reunion circa 1922 at Port Stanley. Courtesy of Margaret (Maggie) May Abbott Shackleton photo album. Standing left rear: Mary Shackleton Rowe, ?, ?, Ruby Abbott Shackleton, John Shackleton, Laura Woolley Shackleton, ?, ?, Hazel Shackleton, ?, Ellen Abbott Houghton, Albert Abbott, ?, ?, ?,? Stewart Shackleton, ?, Earl Row, ?, ?,? Lorne Shackleton, ?, Seated middle row: ?, Thomas Lethbridge Abbott, Priscilla Abbott Baldwin, John R. Abbott, Maggie Abbott Shackleton, Annie Lapthorne Abbott, Sara McCord Abbott, Keith Abbott, Charles Abbott. Seated on ground: ?, ?, ?, ?,?, ?, ?, Dorothy Shackleton, ?, ?, Donald Shackleton, Clayton Shackleton, ?

We know that about 1922 the Abbott Reunion was held at Port Stanley, Ontario. A photograph from Margaret (Maggie) May Abbott Shackleton's photo album shows many of William Abbott's children: Priscilla Abbott Baldwin, John (Jack) and Annie Abbott, possibly Albert and Mary Abbott, Edwin and Harriet Abbott, and Charlie and Sarah Abbott. Although each individual cannot be identified, the next generation was well represented and includes several Shackletons including Laura Woolley Shackleton Campbell, Mary Shackleton and Earl Row, Maggie and Lorne Shackleton, and Ruby and John Shackleton. Many of the children are recognizable: Hazel Shackleton and her brother Stewart, along with Clayton, Donald, and sister, Dorothy, seated on the grass with other very young children. The group of about twenty-five people gathered at the popular beachside picnic area.

For many years in the 1930s, Gladstone School was the home of the reunion. We know from the Reunion Minutes that attendance was strong in the 40s when up to eighty people regularly attended when it was held at Springbank Park in London. In this photo we see a group facing away from the camera but on the right side are Annie and John Abbott seated at the picnic table.

Abbott Reunion, circa 1940 at Springbank Park, London, Ontario. Courtesy of Loreen VanKoughnett and Margaret Dunn.

Minutes of The Abbott-Kingwell Reunion have survived as far back as 1947. They contain descriptions of pot luck buffet lunches; the names of winners of foot races; the youngest and oldest attendees; the names of executives; who nominated whom, who seconded whom; who came the farthest; how much was spent on postage, coffee, and other sundries; and the names of those who had passed away in any given year and were thought of during the "minute of silence". We can see from the Secretary's Report of 1948 that eighty relatives attended that year.

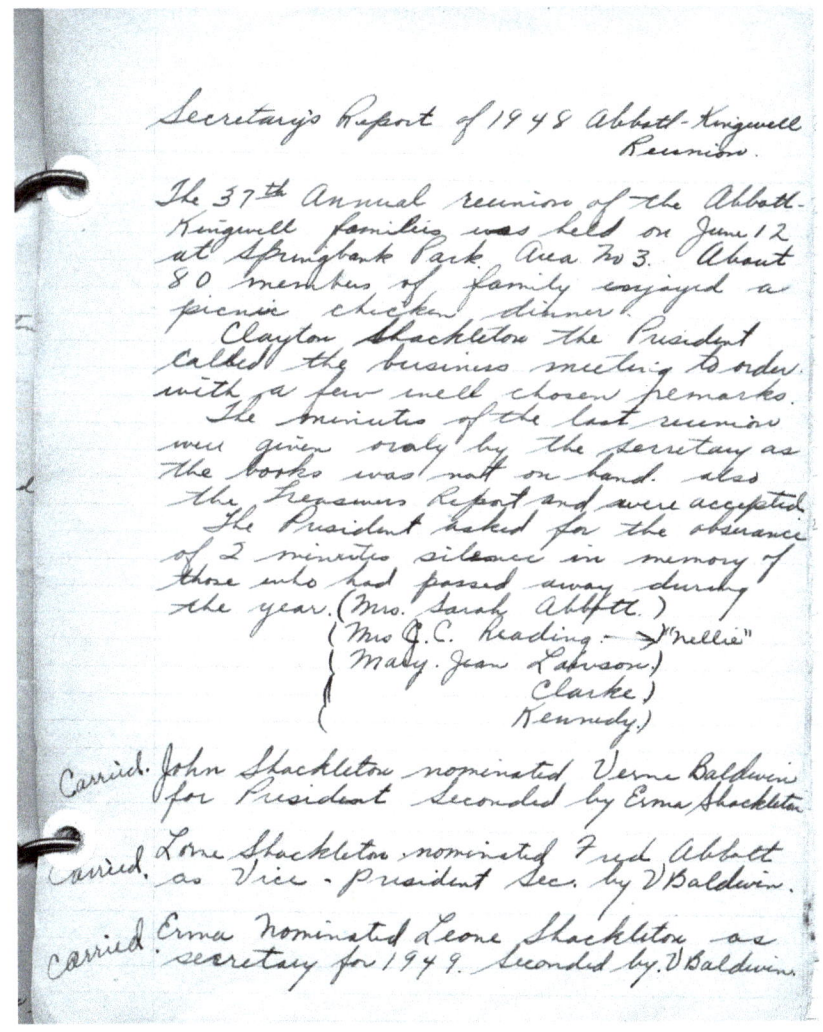

Secretary's Report [Minutes] of 1948 Abbott-Kingwell Reunion.

Like all large families, the Abbotts had their share of joy and sorrow. Each year at the reunion, there is a "minute of silence" to remember those that had passed away since the last reunion. Presidents and their Executives have presided over business meetings where the modest budget has been presented for all to see and hear before the plate was passed around to collect donations for the following year. During the 1930s the takings were slim. The amount spent on postage, a great part of the budget in the 1960s, was not such an issue for the one-hundredth reunion in 2010 when more than half of those invited received their invitation by electronic mail.

Another big decision was always where to hold the gathering the following year and whether to take advantage of the hospitality of a perennial host or try a different location like the pavilion in a local park to try to attract more participants. At times phone committees were established to call long unseen relatives and try to persuade them to attend.

The connection between the Kingwell and Abbott families was forged in 1852 when Mary Ann Abbott married William Kingwell in Plympton St. Mary Parish, Devon, England. Mary Ann's brother, William Abbott, immigrated to Canada in 1871 with his wife Lydia and their eight children. They were accompanied by Mary Ann's son, Philip Kingwell. The Kingwell descendants had joined their Abbott cousins at the annual reunion for many years. Bernard Kingwell, who was raised in Saskatchewan, recalled that in 1941 his family came to the Abbott-Kingwell Reunion which was held that year in London at Wonderland Gardens, made famous by the popular bandleader Guy Lombardo and his Royal Canadians. In fact, throughout the 1940s and 50s Springbank Park was the site of the reunion until 1958 when the annual gathering moved to Pinafore Park in St. Thomas. In 1955 attendance was strong, with ninety attending. However, in the 1960s and 70s attendance fluctuated from twenty to thirty and then at times between eighty-five and one hundred and two. This was the period when many individual families hosted the reunion. In 1974 the Abbotts gathered at Peter and Leta Lawson's home, in 1975 at Ron and Marg Abbott's, in 1976 at Evelyn and Jim McCracken's farm. Les Shackleton hosted for several years in the late 70s at his farm or at the Shackleton Auction Barn in Springfield, Ontario, Robert & Sylvia Shackleton hosted in Paris, Ontario in 1982. Later in the 1980s, the reunion was held at the Avon Community Centre and at Gibbon's Park in London.

Abbott-Kingwell Reunion at Gibbon's Park, London, Ontario, 1985. Photo taken by Cathy Cave. Courtesy of Charles Baldwin. Front row: Jean Houghton, Neil Brown, Randy Brown, Ryan Norrington, Sheila Brown, ?, ?, Marlene Travis, Brad Travis, Sean Travis, Dorothy Garton, ?, ?, ?. Second row: Hazel Ferguson, Ruby Moody, Sylvia Shackleton, Destiny Shackleton, Diane Houghton, Jimmy Houghton, Vernon Houghton, Prudence Kingwell, Estelle Cave, ?, ?, Norine Abbott. Third row: Charlie Baldwin, Robert Shackleton, Dennis Brown holding ?, Russell Houghton, Verne Shackleton, Marlene Baldwin, Judy Brown, Blanche Shackleton, ?, Bernard Kingwell, Nigel Kingwell, Kelly Kingwell, Paul Shackleton, ?, Bonnie Abbott, Don Abbott, ?, ?, ?, ?, Marlyn Cross, Ray Cross, Janet Shackleton holding ?. The photo shows Robert Shackleton holding the Abbott-Kingwell banner with Bernard Kingwell holding the other side.

The following year, the reunion was held at the Avon Community Centre in Avon, Ontario. It was noted in the Reunion minutes that there was a good turnout of fifty-eight people that year with several families represented who had not attended in many years: Eula Abbott Hunt and Lewis Hunt, Elise Abbott Armstrong and family from Wayne, Michigan among them.

When Philip and Sena (Baldwin) Abbott moved to Manitoba in 1911, their daughters married local men and since then generations of their children have called the west their home. They knew little about the Ontario Abbotts except that the Abbott sisters visited back and forth over the years posing for photographs at train stations as they welcomed each other or said their goodbyes. In 2005 the Western Abbotts held their

The Abbott-Kingwell Reunion

first Abbott Reunion at the home of Wayne and Sharon Harland in Winnipeg. I attended that reunion with my husband, Joseph and my mother, Hazel. We connected with so many relatives of our own generation that we had never known before. In 2009, several of Philip Abbott's descendants who were born and raised in Treherne, Manitoba attended the reunion in Glanworth, Ontario.

Abbott Reunion, Winnipeg Manitoba, 2005. Photo Courtesy of Joseph Romain. Front row: Vera Henry Bowles, Hazel Shackleton Ferguson, Ruby Henry Scammell and Gail Ferguson. Second row: Les Shackleton, Don Bowles, Velma Harland, Sydney Maruca, Lorinda Harland Maruca, Robin Scammell Davis, Joanne Henry, Connie Henry, Brenda Rock, Tessa Kidd. Third row: Darren Maruca, Roberta Henry McDonald, Kristi Kidd, Barbara Henry, Joyce Harland and Elaine Wilke. Fourth row: Harvey Harland, Jim Scammell, Brad Harland, Robert Harland, Stan McDonald, Danny Davis, Sheryl Rock, Sharon Harland, Wayne Harland and Reg Wilke.

From the 1990-2005 most of the reunions were held at Thorndale Community Centre and at Gerry & Ruth Abbot's home in Glanworth, Ontario. Then the reunion went back to Gibbon's Park and Pinafore Park a few more times. Attendance varied from year to year and those who came wore name tags to recognize and identify those who were their distant cousins.

Many times throughout the years there was a feeling that the reunion would be discontinued if more people didn't attend. Various attempts were made to increase the numbers: an aggressive campaign of telephone invitations, everyone encouraged to bring someone who hadn't attended the previous year, and so on.

Ultimately the Abbotts and Kingwell descendants returned to Thorndale for the one-hundredth gathering in 2010 where more than one hundred people wore carefully designed name tags made by Charles Baldwin which spelled out the lineage of their particular branch of the Abbott Family.

Name tag from the one hundredth Abbott-Kingwell Reunion. Researched, designed and created by Charles Baldwin.

PRIME MINISTER · PREMIER MINISTRE

It is with great pleasure that I extend my warmest greetings to everyone attending the Abbott-Kingwell family's 100th anniversary reunion.

Today, you have gathered to celebrate the special bond of family. This wonderful tribute allows you to reminisce about your collective history, to share treasured memories and to reconnect with those individuals who have helped shape your lives. You may take great pride in your family's many achievements and in its unique contribution to the vitality of our country.

I wish you all a most enjoyable and memorable reunion.

OTTAWA
2010

Letter of congratulation from The Right Honourable Stephen Harper, Prime Minister of Canada.

At the one hundredth anniversary of the reunion, amidst the letters of congratulation from federal and provincial Members of Parliament and from The Right Honourable Stephen Harper, Prime Minister of Canada, those who were present made an important decision.

It was moved that the families should congratulate themselves on their longstanding tradition, but discontinue the annual reunion for the future as so many of us are only very distantly related anymore and there are very few children attending. There was a prolonged discussion and then came the vote in favour of celebrating the last annual reunion in 2010.

The annual reunion had survived bad weather, lean years, and decreasing numbers of descendants, many of whom had no idea how they were related. At times confused by the exact relationship, they'd attended the reunion with parents, with their young families, or perhaps after the loss of a parent, knowing that somehow they were all related. Were it not for the annual picnic they might have had no knowledge of each other at all. What most of them didn't know was that they shared a connection with William Abbott, a thirty-nine-year-old master blacksmith, who stepped out of his comfort zone and brought his family from Devonshire, England to Ontario, Canada in 1871. He became the father of generations of Abbotts in Canada and beyond. William's nephew, Philip Kingwell, also took a chance and emigrated with his aunt and uncle's family to start a new life in Canada. His brother, Isaac Kingwell, followed a few years later. They settled first in Ontario and then some of the family moved further west and continued the Kingwell line in Herschel, Saskatchewan.

For one hundred years their descendants had met annually to connect as a family. We can be proud of that long tradition as we examine the ancestry of the Abbotts of Devonshire and the new life they made in Canada.

One hundredth Abbott-Kingwell Reunion, Thorndale Ontario, 2010. Courtesy of Charles Baldwin. Front row (seated on the floor behind the banner): Ethyn Brown, Alannah Gosnell, Kayd Brown, Andrew Gosnell. Second row (seated): Destiny Shackleton, Gavin Smith, Bill Shackleton, Ken Shackleton, Eunice Baldwin Tuck, Catherine Cave, Maxine Eveland, Ellison Hunt, Hazel Ferguson, Bernard Kingwell, Sean Kingwell, Nigel Kingwell, Josie Andrada, ?, Dorothy Garton, Diane Burgess, Louise Shackleton, Grace Johnson, Leta Lawson, Loreen Vankoughnett. Third row (standing): Susan Locke, Norma Shackleton, Roger Tuck, Myrna Huff, Verna Stratton, Margaret Shackleton, Brent Shackleton, Wayne Harland, Gail Ferguson, Les Shackleton, Shirley Franklin, Dan Stewart, Heather Franklin, Jerry Zahorodni, Judy Brown, Gary Gill, Ralph Johnson, Irene Johnson, Betty McCracken, Rick McCracken, Charles Baldwin, Margaret Dunn. Fourth row (seated on stage): Susan Sweetman, Stephanie Gosnell, Connie Parsons, Walter Parsons, Christine Shackleton, Sarah Jane Brown, Marlene Baldwin, Joyce Harland, Shaunalee Derkson, Jean Houghton, Diane Houghton, Verne Houghton, Brenda Fletcher, Emily Brown, Marlyn Brady, Shultzee Lonee, Brenda Brain. Fifth row (standing): Brian Sweetman, Tom Gosnell, Leon Parsons, Leonard Parsons, David Brown, Bonnie McGlynn, Doug McGlynn, Bernice Duffin, Bob Duffin, Ron Abbott, Marg Abbott, ?, Scott Fletcher, Launie Fletcher, Bill Brady, ?, Kelly Brain, Janice Brain, Chris Brain and Howard Brain.

The Abbotts

Chapter 2
In Devonshire

William Abbott (1832-1914) and Lydia Lethbridge Abbott (1831-1872) came to Canada in 1871 from Devonshire, England with their eight children: Albert (1855-1929); William (1856-1887); Philip (1858-1934); Edwin (1860-1927); Priscilla (1861-1935); John (1863-1944); Thomas (1867-1925); and Charles (1869-1950). They left behind their parents, their siblings, and a way of life.

This chapter attempts to describe where the Abbotts lived before they emigrated from England. It also explains the ancestral lines of both William Abbott and Lydia Lethbridge to the extent that I have been able to verify their lineage.

The Abbott and Lethbridge families lived in the southern part of the County of Devon, formerly Devonshire, among, rolling hills, shady woodlots, and winding rivers. Small villages were the economic centres that punctuated the rural landscape. Abbott Country is bordered on the north by Dartmoor, the wild and rugged locale of the fictional *Hound of the Baskervilles*; to the west by the busy and prosperous City of Plymouth, a Royal dockyard since 1689 and later a Royal Navy base; to the south and east by the coastal areas of Torquay and Dartmouth, with their fine natural harbours which were so vital to the fishery trade; and connected to its neighbouring counties by the South Devon Railway Line built in the 1840s. The coastline on the English Channel is punctuated by the broad estuaries of rivers like The Yealm, The Erme, The Dart, The Avon, and The Plym which originate in the heights of Dartmoor and navigate their way through rocky gorges, pastoral farmlands and broad dappled curves.

New Map of Devonshire, 1807. We can see Plymouth in the west and Dartmouth to the south-east. Places of importance to Abbott family are marked in red. Courtesy of the David Rumsey Map Collection, www.davidrumsey.com

The British Census of 1871 for Yealmbridge, Devon, was taken on Sunday, April 2, 1871. It provides a snapshot of the Abbott family a mere three months before they arrived in Canada[1]. The Census information shows that William Abbott's occupation was a master blacksmith. His eldest son Albert was also a blacksmith. William, Lydia and seven of their eight children are recorded as having been born in either the Parish of Ermington or Yealmpton. Philip, Edwin, Priscilla and John were about one year apart and attending school. There is a gap of a few years and then Thomas and Charles were born. The second eldest son, William Jr, is not recorded in the list of names of family members. He may have been working, studying or visiting elsewhere on the day the Census was recorded. As Thomas, aged four, was born in Ermington Parish and Charles, aged one, was born in Yealmpton Parish, the family may have lived in Yealmbridge, where they were enumerated, for only a few years. Not long before they made the decision to emigrate.

The Abbotts

Census of England and Wales, 1871. Devon, Yealmpton, Dist. 15, Page 34. The census entry shows the family of William and Lydia Abbott just prior to emigration. Credit: The National Archives of the UK.

Picture the hamlet of Yealmbridge in 1871, located north-east of the village of Yealmpton, in the parish of the same name, Yealmpton[2]. Yealmbridge was a tiny settlement of only seven houses including a smithy (blacksmith's forge) which would have provided work for William Abbott. Its total population of forty souls included an innkeeper, a lime kiln burner, a toll gate collector, a market gardener, a master of sawmills and a retired clergyman. In the surrounding area were two sawmills that provided some employment, but the main village in the area was Yealmpton which had a thriving cattle market and three corn mills. There were few other populated areas on either bank of the River Yealm.

Two miles, as the crow flies, from Yealmbridge was another hamlet in Ermington Parish called Westlake, where the Abbott family had lived in 1861. At that time, William Abbott and Lydia Lethbridge were raising their young family. In the census entry we can see the twenty-eight-year-old head of the family, William, was a blacksmith. Also shown are his wife Lydia, their eldest son, six-year-old Albert, born in Plympton St. Mary

In Devonshire   15

Parish and three younger children: William Jr., Philip and Edwin, all born in Ermington Parish.[3] Ermington Village spread across both banks of the Erme River and was less than a mile to the east along the road. It was a thriving hub with all manner of occupations represented in the Census enumeration. There were shoemakers, boot-binders, several schoolmasters, masons, grocers, lawyers, thatchers, four wheelwrights and a blacksmith shop owned by Philip Coleman and his two sons Nicholas and John who are also smiths. The shop employed several men.

Census of England and Wales, 1861. Devon, Ermington, Dist. 18, Page 4. The census entry shows William and Lydia Abbott and family living at Westlake in Ermington Parish. Credit: The National Archives of the UK.

The Abbotts

THE ABBOTT ANCESTORS

The Abbotts had lived for generations in South Devon. William Abbott's parents were Philip Abbott (1801-1874) and Priscilla Rowse (1805-1892). William Abbott's Grandfather, Roger Abbott (1764-1827), was born in Dean Prior, Devon on May 27, 1764. Roger died in Ermington on Jan. 25, 1827. William's Grandmother, Miriam Metherel (1773-1834), was also born in Dean Prior. She was baptised on June 13, 1773 and died in Ermington on Dec. 11, 1834. Roger Abbott was the son of Richard Abbott (1724-1775). Richard married Mary Phillips (no dates) on March 15, 1751[4]. We have no confirmed evidence of Richard's (1724-1775) parentage, however, there are baptismal records for three of Richard's brothers Roger, Philip and William, all stating that their father's name was Richard Abbott. Richard Abbott (1699-) was born in Buckfastleigh and was baptized on March 2, 1699[5]. He married Jane Pearse (no dates) on January 12, 1724[6]. Five of their male children were born in Dean Prior: Richard (1724-), Roger (1728-), Philip (1731-), William (1734-), and John (1737-). They had two daughters: Grace (1729-) and Mary (1742-). Richard's (1699-) father was William Abbott (no dates)[7]. William married Grace Veal [Gulielmus Abbott and Gratia Veal as written, in Latin, on the marriage registration] on the 13th of June 1693 in Buckfastleigh[8]. William and Grace appear to have had at least three children: Joane (Dec 14-29th, 1695)[9], Mary (1697-)[10], and Richard (1699-). William's (no dates) father may have been William Abbott of Buckfastleigh, born on May 2, 1614. There was a William Abbotte who was baptised in Honiton-on-Otter, Devon on May 8, 1614. The relationship between these two William Abbotts was suggested by Bernard Kingwell, but we have found no document that confirms that one was the father of the other. William (1614-) is the earliest generation of Abbotts found so far in this research. So it is possible that he is the father of all subsequent generations as Honiton-on-Otter is roughly a half day walk from Buckfastleigh.

In Devonshire

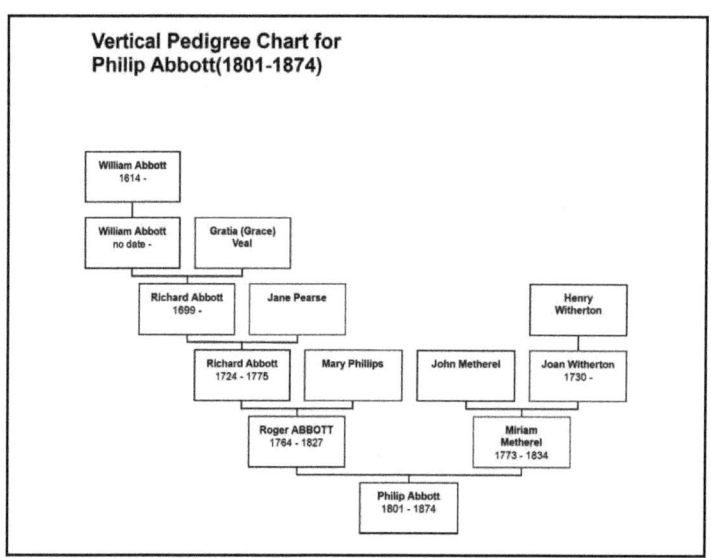

Pedigree chart of Philip Abbott (1801-1874)

Genealogical research about Roger Abbott (1764-1827), the Grandfather of William Abbott who immigrated to Canada, indicates that William may not have been the first Abbott to cross the Atlantic. The marriage oath of Roger Abbott and Miriam Metherel indicates that Roger, as Master of a cod fishing ship, had sailed to North America from Devon on a "Newfoundland" ship:

> *Roger Abbott late Master of the "Nagdown" Newfoundland ship appeareth personally and make oath, that He is an unmarried man upwards of Twenty-one years of age and not related within the forbiden degrees to Miriam Metherell (sic) of Ermington for the marriage of whom, with him the said Roger Abbott License is prayed. And John Metherel, brother of the said, Miriam, maketh Oath, and saith, that the said Miriam Metherel is an unmarried woman upwards of Twenty one years of age and that she hath had her usual abode during four weeks last past within the Parish of Ermington. And the aforesaid Roger Abbott on his Oath saith that he knows no just Cause why he, the said Roger Abbott may not be lawfully married to the said Miriam Metherell (sic).*
>
> *Signed Roger Abbott, John Meatherel*
> *Sworn before me this 25th day of February, 1796. John [Gandy...] Surrogate*

The marriage oath document of Roger Abbott and Miriam Metherel. 1796. Credit: Plymouth & West Devon Record Office.

In Devonshire

The Newfoundland fishing trade was of major importance to the economy of Devon throughout the eighteenth and nineteenth centuries. Villages such as Shaldon near Teignmouth and Kingswear near Dartmouth were inhabited almost exclusively by families dependent on the Newfoundland fishery. Newton Abbot, an inland market town in South Devon, was a major recruiting centre for both the Teignmouth and Dartmouth commercial fishing fleets and was home to families who depended on the Newfoundland trade. In 1809 a visitor to Newton Abbot reported that "Sixteen Captains of Ships which sailed to Newfoundland...resided with their families at the place," and that "at the season appointed for hiring there have been 1200 Sailors assembled in the town to be hired."[11] Dean Prior, the birthplace of Roger Abbott, was a four-hour walk to this important employment market.[12] Roger would have risen to the position of Master of a commercial ship after several years as a seaman. As the fishing boats left from Devon ports in the spring, carrying locally made supplies such as iron nails and tools, ropes, baskets, etc. to the fishery bases in Newfoundland, Roger would have been away for much of the summer, returning in the fall with the boats and their bounty of salt cod. The children of Roger and Miriam were born in 1799 (William), 1801 (Philip), 1803 (Emmaline), and 1815 (John). They would have come along during the stretch of years when Roger was at home in Ermington, punctuated by periods at sea.

If we can indulge indirect evidence for a moment, we can trace a circuitous connection between William Abbott and Lydia Lethbridge in their direct ancestral lines. Let's consider the ancestry of Miriam Metherel (1773-1834), the wife of Roger Abbott (1764-1827). Miriam was baptised in Dean Prior Parish on June 13, 1773. According to the baptismal records of the parish her parents were John Metherel and Joan [Witherton][13]. A John Metherel (no dates) and Joan Witherton (1730-) were married in Dean Prior Parish on March 29, 1752. Joan's father was Henry Witherton (1700-), also of Dean Prior. Miriam's brother, John Metherel (1765-1830), who vouched for her in the marriage oath (above) subsequently married Joanna Medland and eventually became the father of Elizabeth Metherel (1796-1859) who was to marry Thomas Lethbridge (1796-1861), the father of Lydia Lethbridge (1831-1872), William Abbott's first wife. Therefore, William and Lydia were second cousins through their grandparents, Miriam and John Metherel, who were siblings. These close relationships were very common in underpopulated rural communities and they were one of the reasons why marriage oaths were so relied upon to ensure that the bride and groom were not too closely related by consanguinity or affinity[14].

Woolwork picture of a 3-masted fishing ship from the Henley Collection, Dartmouth Museum, Dartmouth, Devon.

THE ROWSE ANCESTORS

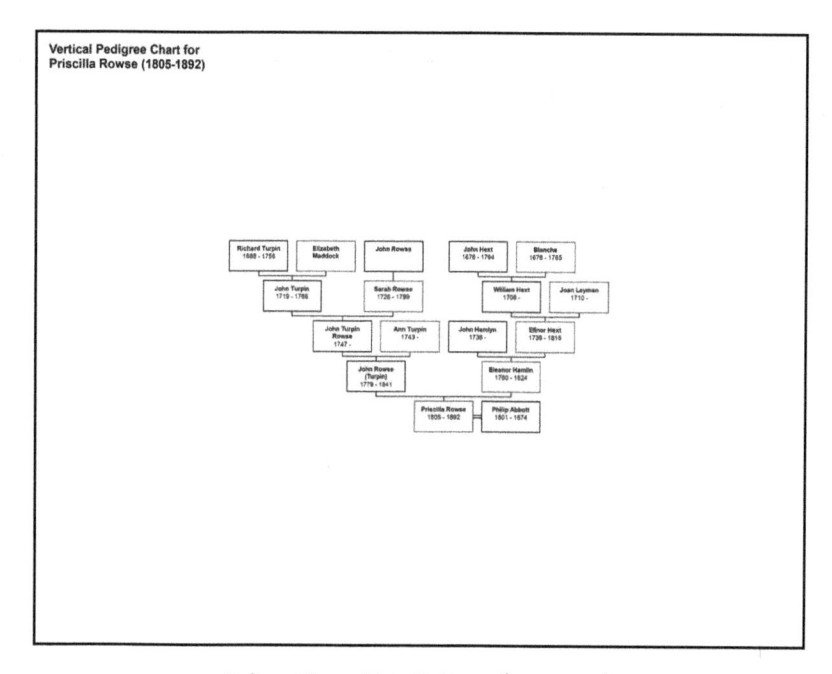

Pedigree Chart of Priscilla Rowse (1805-1892)

William Abbott's mother was Priscilla Rowse (1805-1892). She was the daughter of John Rowse Turpin (1779-1841) and Eleanor Hamlyn (1780-1824). Although their father's name is John Rowse Turpin, Priscilla and her siblings bear the surname Rowse. It's interesting that these children were named Rowse rather than Turpin. Research suggests that this was the result of a birth out of wedlock several generations back. Priscilla's father, John Rowse Turpin (1779-1841), was the son of John Turpin Rowse (1747-1821) and Ann Turpin (1743-1813). John Turpin Rowse (1747-1821) was the son of John Turpin (1719-1786) and Sarah Rowse (1726-1799). There is no marriage record found for a marriage between John and Sarah. John Turpin (1719-1786) married Priscilla Maddock in 1748, the year following the birth of John Turpin Rowse, his son by Sarah Rowse. The lack of a marriage record and several family tree entries of people researching the Rowse family suggests that John Turpin Rowse was born out of wedlock. John Turpin (1719-1786) then married, and had thirteen children, with his wife, Priscilla Maddock. Sarah Rowse later married James Sampson in 1855 and had two children with the surname Sampson. With fifteen half brothers and sisters, John Turpin Rowse was one illegitimate son among many legitimate siblings. One could understand that he held on to his mother's surname, Rowse, and was referred to as John Turpin Rowse, indicating that his father's surname was Turpin.

John Turpin Rowse (1747-1821) married for the first time to Grace Matthews on January 23, 1774, and they had one child, Mary Rowse, born in 1774 before Grace died in 1776. The plot thickened when John Turpin Rowse married his second wife, Ann Turpin (1743-1813), on August 2, 1778, in Plympton St. Mary Parish.

John Turpin Rowse and Ann Turpin marriage record 1778. Credit: Plymouth & West Devon Record Office.

The marriage of two people with the same family name, "Turpin", is curious. One family chart, states that Ann's maiden name was Biddex and that she had been married previously to another John Turpin. However, as the marriage registration says "Ann Turpin, Spinster", I believe it is more likely that she was also a descendant of the large Turpin family and may have been a not so distant cousin to John Turpin Rowse. There is definitely room for further research here. One family tree indicates that John and Ann had six children: John Rowse (1779- 1841), Mary (1782-), Priscilla (1784-), Ann (1786-), Grace (1789-), and James Hele (1790-).

In Devonshire

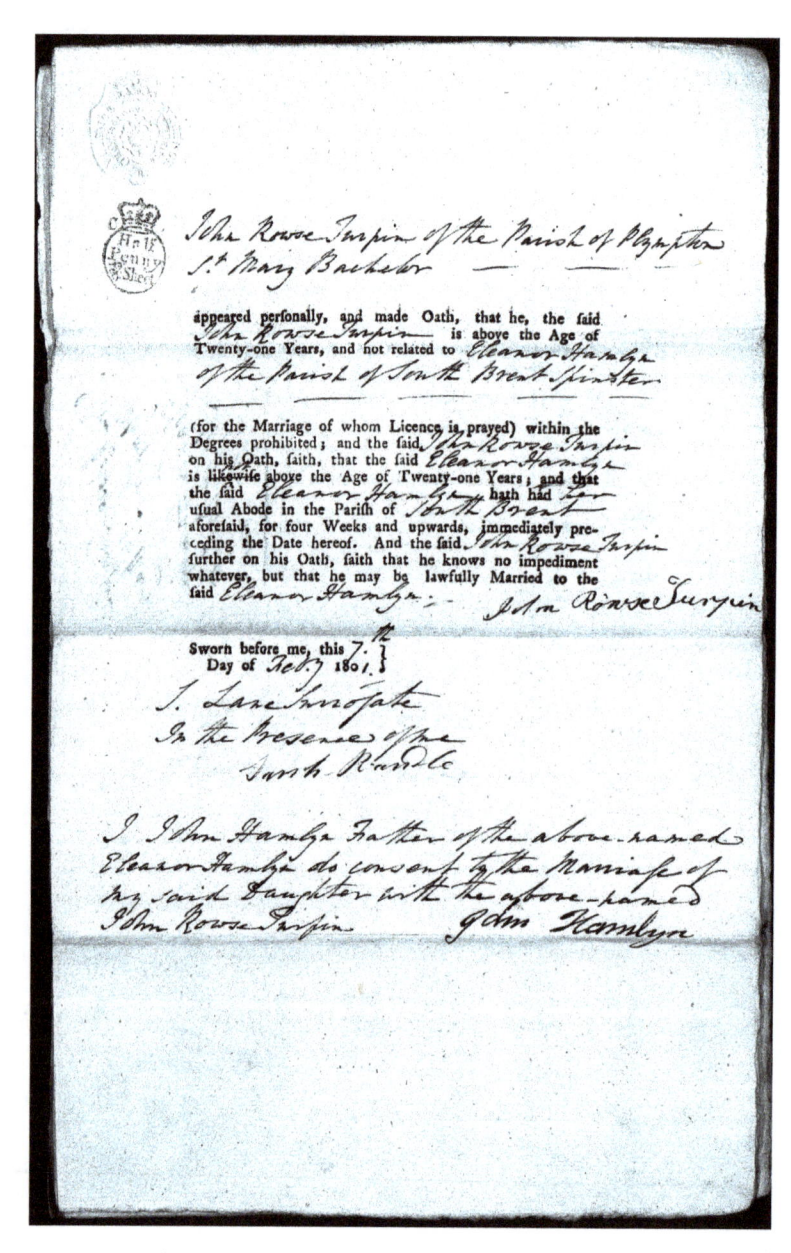

John Rowse Turpin and Eleanor Hamlyn marriage oath 1801.
Credit: Plymouth & West Devon Record Office.

John Rowse Turpin (1779-1841) and Eleanor Hamlyn (1780-1824) were the parents of Priscilla Rowse (1805-1892). When they married on February 13, 1801, the wedding took place in South Brent, Devon where Eleanor was born on March 7, 1780. Eleanor's father was John Hamlyn or Hamlin, or Hamblyn. Her mother was Elinor Hext. As Eleanor had not yet reached the age of majority, John Rowse Turpin and Eleanor Hamlyn had to agree to a marriage oath which stated that Eleanor's father swore that he gave his permission for his daughter to marry.

According to several family trees[15], John and Eleanor Rowse had eleven children: James Hele (1800-), John Hamblyn (1802-), Eleanor (1804-), Priscilla (1805-), Mary (1807-), Ann (1809-), Joseph Henry (1810-), William (1812-), Richard (1814-), Eliza Hamblyn (1816-) and Mary Ann (1817-). Following Eleanor`s death in 1824, John wed for a second time marrying Bridget Gardiner in 1825. Bridget may have had a daughter, Mary West, by an earlier relationship.

The Rowse name appears often in generations of Abbott descendants. William Abbott and Lydia Lethbridge named their fifth son John Rowse Abbott. The Rowse connection prevails later in Ontario where we find neighbours of the Abbotts in North Dorchester, named Rowse. One, in fact, John Lethbridge Rowse was the first cousin of William Abbott through William`s mother Priscilla and to Lydia Lethbridge through her father Thomas Lethbridge.

WILLIAM ABBOTT'S FAMILY IN DEVON

William Abbott (1832-1914) was born in Lee Mill Bridge on May 13, 1832, he was christened one month later in Ivybridge in the non-conformist Wesleyan Methodist faith[16]. His father, Philip Abbott, was listed as a blacksmith in the Methodist Register. His mother, Priscilla, and her parents, John and Eleanor Rowse, are mentioned in his baptismal registration.

William was raised in the Village of Lee Mill Bridge where he eventually apprenticed as a blacksmith. In the Census of 1841[17], William Abbott's parents, Philip and Priscilla Abbotts (sic), appear in Lee Mill Bridge, with Philip working as a smith along with two unrelated males Stephen Life, age fifty and John Bowden, age fifteen, both smiths, or assistants. At this time, William Abbott was nine years of age. Philip and Priscilla were recorded with their large family of seven children at a time when Priscilla was only thirty years of age. She

In Devonshire

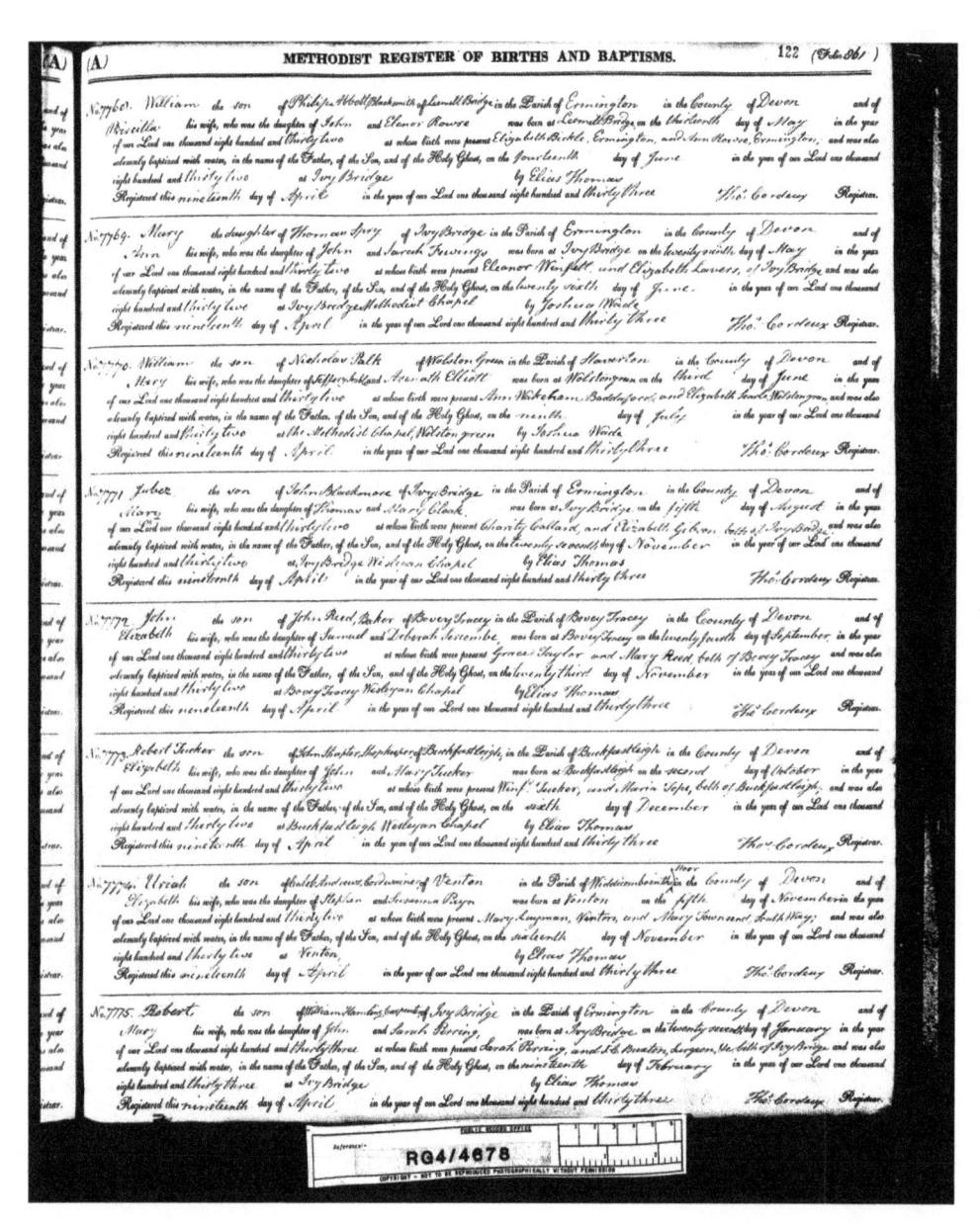

William Abbott baptismal registration England & Wales Non-Conformist and Non-Parochial Registers, 1567-1970. Piece 4678: Wesleyan Metropolitan Registry, Paternoster Row, 1794-1834. Credit: The National Archives of the UK.

bore her eldest child, Emmaline (Emily), at the age of fifteen. This Census entry made on June 6, 1841, lists a child, John, age one year, who died four years later in 1845.

Census of England and Wales, 1841. District, Plympton St Mary, Sub-registration district: Yealmpton. Showing Philip and Priscilla Abbotts (sic) and family. Credit: The National Archives of the UK.

In the 1851 Census, enumerated on March 30, 1851, William's enumerated siblings were Mary Ann, age twenty-one; a younger brother, Philip age sixteen, who was also a blacksmith's apprentice; a sister Miriam age twelve who was at school; and another sibling, Ellen or Eleanor age four[18]. The head of the family, William's father, Philip, was described as a master blacksmith and victualer, (a supplier of food and drink and, in Britain, a licensed purveyor of spirits, or an innkeeper) and William's mother, Priscilla, was an innkeeper's wife.

Census of England and Wales, 1851. District, Plympton St Mary, Sub-district 4b. Showing the Philip Abbott family in 1851. Credit: The National Archives of the UK.

A survey of the whole of England and Wales was undertaken in the decade or so after 1836, to establish the boundaries of each parish, and assess the amount of tithe due for each parcel of land within it. *The Tithe Apportionment* for Plympton St. Mary Parish, dated 1840[19], shows that Philip Abbott owned several small parcels of land at the centre of Lee Mill Bridge. Plot number 992, a garden, and plot number 997, an orchard, were owned and occupied by Philip Abbott. Plot number 996, a millhouse and garden, was owned by Philip, but occupied by Richard Mumford. Plot number 995, a house and garden, was also owned by Philip but occupied by John Rowe and John Willis.

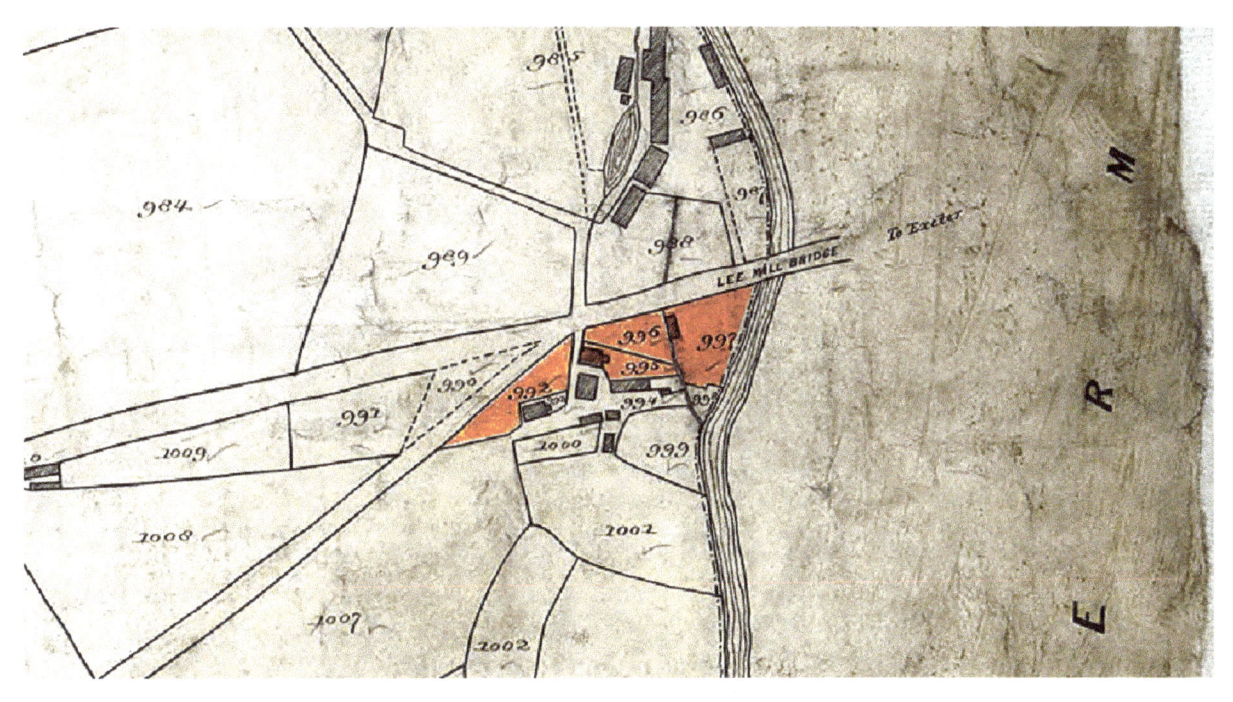

Tithe Apportionment Map showing the plots of land owned by Philip Abbott. Credit: Devon Archives and Local Studies Service.

These plots provided the land for the construction of the Smiths Arms Inn sometime between 1841 and 1852 as shown on the Ordnance Survey of that period below. Philip Abbott owned the land and later ran a blacksmithing business, probably situated behind the inn by 1851. The 1851 Census noted that Philip and Priscilla Abbott "attend to the Inn" although the 1841 Census entry says Philip is a blacksmith and the inn is not mentioned. The Smiths Arms Inn almost certainly got its name from the black*smith*, Philip Abbott, who owned the building and ran the inn with his wife, Priscilla.

William Abbott's father Philip Abbott's occupation as a blacksmith and licensed victualler bears further examination in the context of the village in which he lived. William Abbott's Great Great Grandson, Kevin Shackleton, visited Lee Mill Bridge, Devon in the year 2000, more than one hundred years after William and Lydia immigrated to Ontario. He found a charming village with modern conveniences that gave some indication of the Abbott's livelihood and of the place they called home. During his walk around the village, Kevin

In Devonshire

recalled meeting a man on the street who, when asked if he knew of the Abbott Family, said that they used to run the inn and had an apple orchard behind the inn from which they manufactured cider.

The author visited Lee Mill Bridge in 2018. As I explored around the inn and among the houses and gardens behind it, I found several cottages built at a perpendicular angle to the inn, all having long gardens behind them. The parking lot for the inn ran parallel to these backyards and the pavement stretched eastward as far as the banks of the River Yealm. The tithe map clearly shows a building on the west side of lot 997. This may have been the family's residence before the inn was constructed.

The Smiths Arms Inn is now known as The Westward Inn. It has been renovated several times since the years when the Abbotts lived there. Additions have been built on the eastern and western sides of the stone buildings which housed the original inn. A public house still occupies the main floor and there are rooms above that are no longer used for paying lodgers. The current proprietor provided a tour of the basement where I saw stone walls which were about two feet thick. There were two lintels on the east side and one large arched opening on the west side of the building. Both the east and west walls in the original basement are exterior walls. The additional basement spaces were added on at a later date. The basement of the inn was a likely location for the cider press. Apples from the orchard behind the inn would have been brought into the basement through one of the doorways and pressed into cider to be served in the inn. As cider is a well-known beverage associated with Devon and Cornwall, this operation would have kept the inn supplied with a drink that was as popular then as it remains today.

The blacksmithing forge may have been located behind the inn in the space which is now built upon by a stucco-covered addition to the inn. A sluiceway present in the 1886 Ordnance Survey map, below, would have been used to supply water to the forge, but has been closed off from the river bank and paved over under the present day parking lot.

The Westward Inn viewed from the west side along the Plymouth Road through Lee Mill Bridge. Photo courtesy of the author.

Cottages along The Avenue, formerly called Abbott Row, leading behind the inn off the Plymouth Road. Photo courtesy of the author.

Gardens, formerly an orchard, behind the Westward Inn. Photo courtesy of the author.

The River Yealm flowing under Lee Mill Bridge, adjacent to Westward Inn. Photo courtesy of the author.

The Westward Inn interior main floor. Photo courtesy of the author.

The Westward Inn basement looking through the large arch showing the extent of the cider press area. Photo courtesy of the author.

After the construction of the inn, Ordnance Survey maps from 1841-52, 1886 and 1906 revealed that there were few changes to the adjacent properties. However, the term "Smithy" appears in the earliest map, 1841-52, (shown below), indicating that the forge had been built prior to that time. It was located behind the Smith Arms (P.H.) [public house] constructed along the main street and down the lane to where the row houses stood. Each of the surveys, including the 1886 view, (shown below), indicates that a sluiceway ran from the River Yealm, around the orchard and ending at the mill house. The sluiceway supplied the forge with water from the river that could be controlled as needed. The presence of several trees on each of the surveys indicates the continuing presence of an orchard.

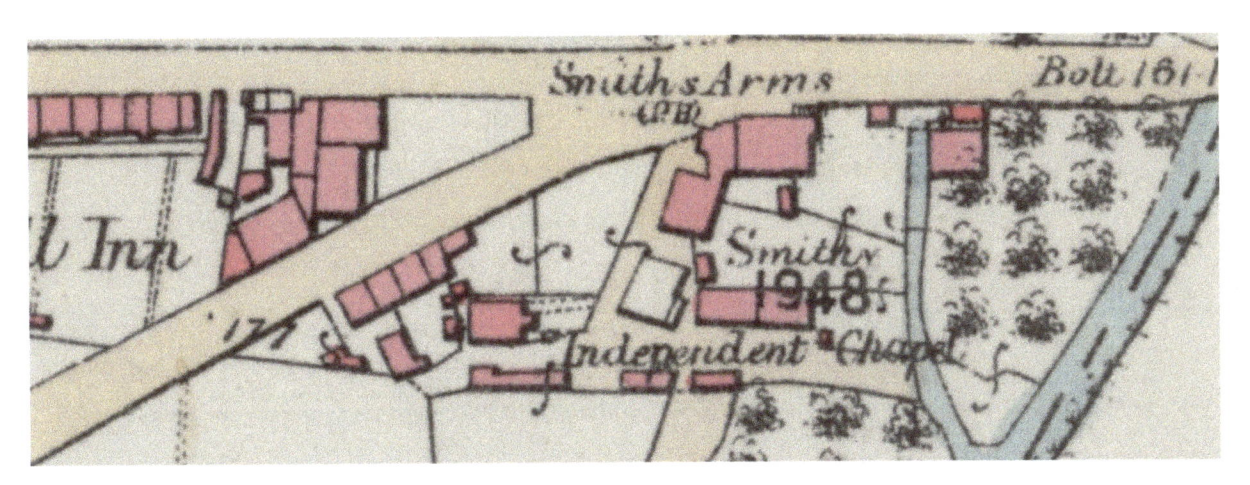

Lee Mill Bridge, Devon as shown in 1841-52 Ordnance Survey. Credit: National Library of Scotland.

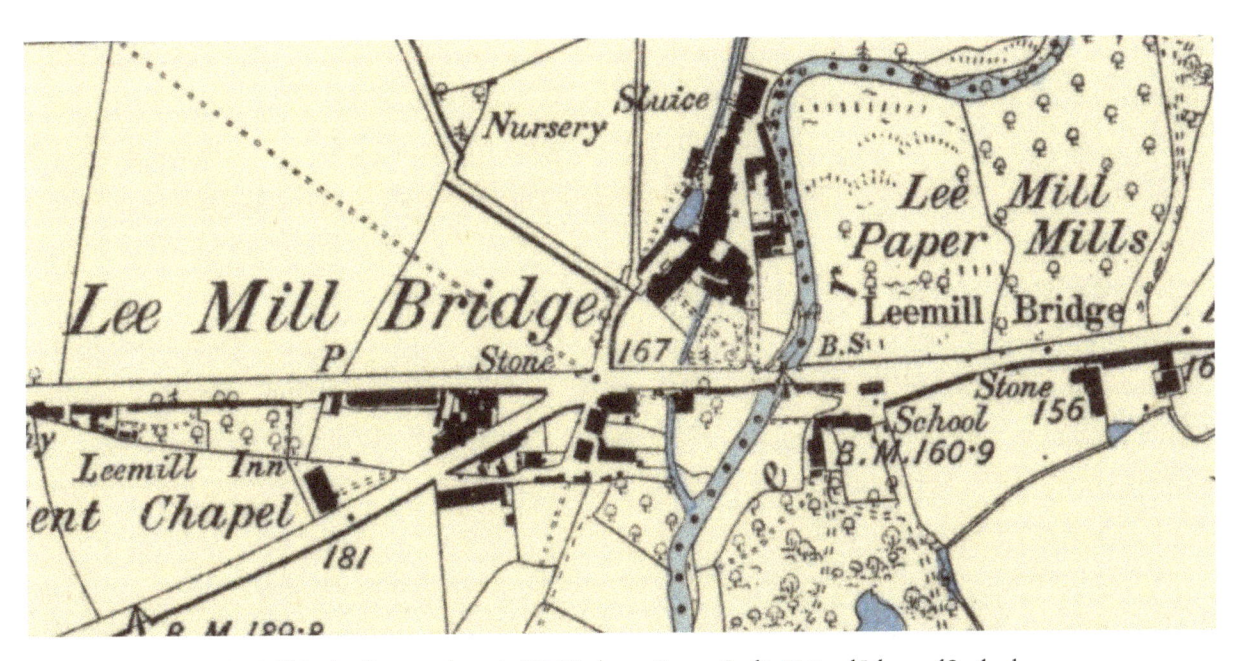

Lee Mill Bridge, Devon as shown in 1886 Ordnance Survey. Credit: National Library of Scotland.

In Devonshire

Bernard Kingwell researched and published a family history of the Abbotts in 1985 *The Abbott Family Tree: Devon England to first generation born in Canada*[20]. He spent many years researching the connection between the Abbott and Kingwell families. He researched all of William Abbott's siblings as well as many generations of ancestors. The following information is from Bernard Kingwell's book:

William's sister, Emmaline Abbott (1825-1906), was born on Jan. 30, 1825 in Plympton. She married Edwin Traher in 1849. They had no children. Edwin died in 1865. Emmaline lived with and kept house for, her widowed brother-in-law Robert Yeoman and his two sons.

William's sister, Priscilla Abbott (1826-1910), was born on Dec. 21, 1826 in Ermington. She married William Sandover in 1848. Sandover was a wheelwright and Priscilla was a dressmaker. They had one child, Ellen, who later married a Blackmore.

William's sister, Mary Ann (1830-1917), was born on Mar 11, 1830, in Ermington. She married William Kingwell on Jan. 11, 1852. They had a large family by 1871: Philip, Emmaline, Isaac, James, Frances, Miriam, and Ellen. Philip Kingwell immigrated to Canada with his uncle, William Abbott. Isaac Kingwell followed his brother to Canada in the 1890s. Both Mary Ann and William Kingwell lived well into their eighties in Ermington.

William's brother, Philip (1834-1920), was born on Sept. 9, 1834, in Ermington. He married Harriet Hamlyn Horton in 1863. Her brother, William Horton, had worked for the Abbott's as an apprentice blacksmith. Philip and Harriet lived next to Philip's parents in what was known as Abbotts Cottage in Lee Mill Bridge. Their children were Beatrice, Alfred, Clara, Maurice and Blanche.

William's sister, Miriam (1838-1881), was born on Nov. 19, 1838 in Ermington. She married Robert Yeoman. Miriam and Robert were married in 1868 and lived in Kingsteignton, Devon. They had a daughter, Blanche, who was born in 1870, but died in 1871. They had a son, Alfred, born in 1873, and a second son, Francis, born in 1874. Miriam died at the relatively young age of forty-three. Robert was a carpenter and a builder and their sons apprenticed as carpenters.

William's brother, John Rowse, was born in 1840. He died within five years in 1845.

William's sister, Eleanor or Ellen (1847-1930), was born in 1847. She lived with her parents, and later with her mother until her mother's death in 1892. At her death in 1930, Eleanor left an estate of over 1,100 British pounds in personal effects.

The Abbotts

The Census entry for Lee Mill Bridge for 1871 shows the residents of the "Smiths Arms Inn": Philip Abbott, age sixty-nine, head of the family, "Blacksmith and Licensed Victualer" along with his wife Priscilla, daughter Eleanor and a servant, Georgina. Their neighbours in "Abbotts Cottage" were William's younger brother, Philip Abbott (1834-1920), thirty-six, his wife Harriet Horton Abbott and four of their five children. Philip Abbott (1834-1920) would eventually run the blacksmith forge and the cider production after the death of his father Philip Abbott (1801-1874). The residents of "Abbotts Row" appear not to be related.

Census of England and Wales, 1871, Devon, Plympton St. Mary Dist.2, page 12. Showing the residents of the Inn and their neighbours in Abbott's Cottage. Credit: The National Archives of the UK.

I am interested in the fact that William, the eldest son, lived, and presumably worked, in Yealmbridge in 1871, while Philip Abbott, William's younger brother, lived and worked on the family property at the Abbotts Cottage. Was the property too crowded for William's large family and they chose to live elsewhere? Was William independent and not willing to work along with his father at the inn and the smithy? Was the smithy too small

In Devonshire   39

to accommodate William's eldest sons, who were apprenticing as blacksmiths themselves? As William and Lydia made the decision to emigrate, was there some amount of friction between father and son, brother and brother? We will never know the answers, but the questions are worth posing.

Three years after William and Lydia immigrated to Canada, Philip Abbott died on Nov. 1, 1874. Upon his death, Philip left a modest estate of less than 300 British pounds in his will[21] which was executed by his son Philip Abbott (1834-1920), blacksmith. Many Devon Wills were lost during the bombing of Exeter during WWII, and Philip's will doesn't seem to have survived, however, his wife, Priscilla, continued to live at the inn for another twenty years until she died in 1892 at the age of eighty-seven. She continued to operate the inn with the help of her son, Philip, and her daughters Eleanor and Priscilla Abbott Sandover who lived at the inn with her husband William Sandover, a retired wheelwright.

The 1891 Census indicates that the Smiths Cottages (formerly called Abbotts Cottage) and the Smithy were next door and were rented to the schoolmistress Sarah Nicholls. When his wife, Harriet, died in 1892, Philip (1834-1920) married the schoolmistress, Sarah Nicholls and yet another Philip Abbott (1901-1903) was added to the family. Next door to the Smiths Inn was the Water Wheel Cottage where a woman named Elizabeth Rowse, likely a niece of Priscilla Rowse Abbott, lived and worked as a flour and meal dealer[22]. Coincidentally, of the many related Abbotts in Lee Mill Bridge and environs, Alfred James Abbott (1865-1950), a grandson of Philip Abbott (1801-1874), lived at Riverside Bungalow on the River Yealm. He operated "The Pub" and employed workers as both a blacksmith and as a publican (British Census of 1911). The tradition continued with Alfred's son, Albert Philip (1895-1966), who worked as a cider manufacturer[23]. The produce of the orchard, therefore, supplied generations of Abbotts who remained in Lee Mill Bridge working as blacksmiths and innkeepers.

LYDIA LETHBRIDGE'S FAMILY IN DEVON:

Lydia Lethbridge was born on February 11, 1831, at Woodland Farm in Devon. Her parents were Thomas Lethbridge (1796-1861) and Elizabeth Metherel (1796-1859). The Lethbridge family lived on the next farm to the widower William Metherel (1795-) of Woodland Farm, the brother of Elizabeth Metherel Lethbridge. Thomas and Elizabeth had seven children: Albert (1826-), Laura (1828-1915), Elizabeth (1829-1887), Lydia (1831-1872), Frederic (1835-6), Thomas (1839-1909) and Sophia (1843-4). No baptismal or death record has been found for Frederic, although his name and dates are found on a tombstone along with others in the family plot.[24] Lydia was baptized less than one month after her birth at the Methodist Chapel in Ivybridge. She has been referred to as Lydia Miriam, but I have not been able to find any documents that confirm this second name[25].

Lydia Lethbridge baptismal registration. Credit: The National Archives of the UK.

Thomas Lethbridge (1796-1861) was the son of Christopher Lethbridge (1760-1827) and Sapience Medland (1763-1806). Christopher Lethbridge had three wives: Joan Jenney Seccombe (1761–1791), Sapience Medland (1763–1806) and Susanna Millin (1795-). There were thirteen children from these marriages. Christopher Lethbridge owned several properties in South Devon. His will refers to his home, Godwell House, in Ugborough, Devon, a fine six bedroom house which was on the real estate market in 2018 for 600,000 British pounds. Godwell House is pictured below. Thomas Lethbridge (1796-1861) received a bequest of 500 British pounds in his father's will.

Godwell House, Ivybridge, Devon. Photo courtesy of www.onthemarket.com, 2018.

The Abbotts

Thomas Lethbridge married Sarah Windeatt on Feb 6, 1821. Their daughter Sarah Windeatt Lethbridge was born on June 22, 1821. Both mother and child died in 1822 and are buried in St. George's Churchyard in Modbury Devon. Elizabeth Metherel (1796-1859) was the second wife of Thomas Lethbridge. They married on Oct 19, 1826, in Ermington. Elizabeth Metherel Lethbridge was the daughter of John Metherel (1765-1830) and Johanna Medland (1766-1822).

When the British Census of 1841 was recorded Lydia Lethbridge was eleven years old. Her parents Thomas and Elizabeth and their surviving children Albert, Laura, Elizabeth, Lydia and Thomas lived in Woodland Village a small hamlet of only eleven families, just east of Lee Mill Bridge. Woodland Village supported a wheelwright, tailor, carpenter, nursery and a butcher as well as several yeomen such as Thomas Lethbridge who owned or at least leased their own land. According to the Tithe Apportionments Thomas owned about forty acres of land at Woodland Farm which he occupied and cultivated in the 1840s.[26] Thomas and Elizabeth must have been relatively prosperous having employed the several labourers who lived at Woodland Farm. Elizabeth Lethbridge appears below in the Census entry[27] with her five children and the agricultural labourers they employed, John Ward, Richard and Eliza Williams and their two children.

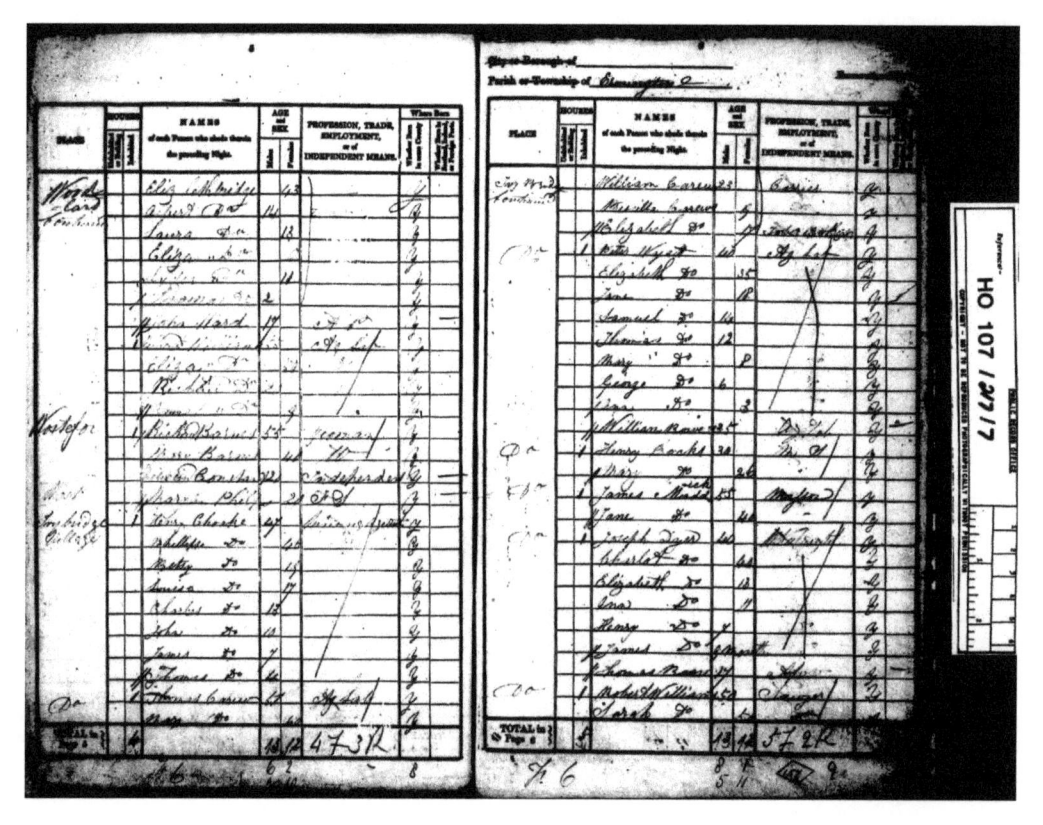

Census of England and Wales, 1841, Devon, Ermington. Elizabeth Lethbridge and family. Credit: The National Archives of the UK.

In the British Census of 1851 Lydia's parents, Thomas and Elizabeth Metherel Lethbridge appear with their family at Cadleigh Farm[28]. Thomas is described as a "Yeoman" with a large 220-acre farm and employing ten men, including Edward Barons, a timber merchant who was married to their daughter Elizabeth. The eldest son Albert was twenty-four, Lydia was twenty, and Thomas age twelve were at home. One daughter Laura did not marry and may have been working in service.

Census of England and Wales, 1851, Devon, Ermington, Page 304. Lethbridge family. Credit: The National Archives of the UK.

    Bert Nelson, a commentator on Rootsweb, a genealogical website, describes a "yeoman" as "farmers (sic) who owned some land or held long term leases (for the lifetime of the father and the son) on lands from the local lord….they were far from landed gentry, but perhaps …their place was somewhere between the gentleman and your average farmer". This may well have been the case for Thomas Lethbridge who appears to have leased the land that he occupied and cultivated at Cadleigh from the family of Rev. Samuel Winter Pearce and his descendants.[29]

Road sign at Cadleigh. Photo courtesy of the author.

Known as Cadleigh Manor, the home and outbuildings still stand. They have been restored and are run as a charming Bed & Breakfast stop for West Country tourists[30]. The author stayed at Cadleigh Manor Bed & Breakfast in September of 2018 for several days using the same main floor rooms at the front of the house that the Lethbridge family would have occupied. The property slopes uphill from the narrow main road between Ivybridge and the intersection of the road to Lee Mill Bridge.

Presently at Cadleigh Farm, several stone farm buildings have been converted into residential homes, while the main bed and breakfast residence has domestic storage buildings behind it which are used for small scale artisanal charcuterie and butchery. The land rises further into pasture, dotted with chicken and duck pens and scattered fruit tree orchards. These are the low rolling farmlands that eventually climb to the heights of the southern edge of Dartmoor.

Cadleigh Manor property as seen from Upper Cadleigh Lane, c. 2018. Photo courtesy of the author.

Cadleigh Farm buildings converted to residential dwellings, c.2018. Photo courtesy of the author.

In Devonshire

Cadleigh Farm buildings and pasture. Photo courtesy of the author.

The history of Cadleigh Farm goes back to 1350 when it was originally a Manor, a landed estate of a feudal lordship, within which, the lord had the right to exercise certain privileges, exact certain fees, etc. In 1826 it was enlarged to create Cadleigh House and was leased until 1891 when it was offered for sale according to a notice in The Times (London) on June 12, 1891[31]. A description of the property can be seen in the notice of the auction sale, below. It was divided into several lots which comprised different parts of the Cadleigh property. Cadleigh House and Farm comprising 274 acres in Lot 1.

> **Ivybridge, South Devon — Freehold Residential Property and valuable Landed Estates for Sale.**
>
> MR. JOHN B. BODY has been instructed to SELL by AUCTION, at Chubb's Hotel, Plymouth, on Thursday, July the 2d, 1891, at 4 o'clock in the afternoon precisely, in the undermentioned lots, and subject to the conditions which will be then produced, copies of which can be obtained of the Auctioneer, or the undermentioned Solicitors, all that FREEHOLD RESIDENTIAL ESTATE, Farm, and Lands known as Cadleigh, situate in the parish of Ermington, in the county of Devon, comprising a well-arranged and commodious residence, with lawn, shrubbery, gardens, and all necessary out-offices; also a Farm Dwelling-house and compact and recently-built farm buildings, and about 319 acres (more or less) of productive meadow, pasture, orchard, and arable land; also of that desirable and attractive Freehold Estate, with a convenient Dwelling-house known as Broomhill and Torlands, situate in the parish of Harford, in the county of Devon, containing about 144½ acres of watered meadow, pasture, and arable land, with extensive rights of common.
>
> | | A. | R. | P. |
> |---|---|---|---|
> | Lot 1.—Cadleigh-house, lawn, shrubbery, &c., and Cadleigh Farm | 274 | 3 | 2 |
> | Lot 2.—All that Pasture Field known as West Cadleigh-park | 4 | 2 | 30 |
> | Lot 3.—All those Two Pasture Fields known as East Cadleigh-park and Hearyland | 9 | 2 | 15 |
> | Lot 4.—All those Six Fields known as Chapleys and Rookery parks, also Kingsfield Plantations, situate close to Lee Mill-bridge | 30 | 0 | 20 |
> | Lot 5.—Broomfield Farm and Torlands | 144 | 1 | 2 |
>
> The property is situate about two miles from the Ivybridge Station on the Great Western Railway, about nine miles from Plymouth and 13 miles from the borough and market town of Totnes.
>
> The Dartmoor Foxhounds and the Modbury Harriers hunt in the neighbourhood, and there is good fishing very near, on the Erme, the Avon, and the Dart, which are preserved rivers.
>
> To a gentleman desirous of farming his own property an opportunity, such as rarely occurs, is afforded for purchasing an estate with a suitable residence in a delightful neighbourhood.
>
> To view apply Cadleigh Farmhouse and Broom-hill Farmhouse respectively.
>
> Plan and particulars, with conditions of sale, may be obtained of the Auctioneer, at Old Town-chambers, Plymouth; or of Messrs. Roober, Matthews, Harrison, and Co., Solicitors, Frankfort-street, Plymouth.—Dated May 30th, 1891.

Advertisement of the sale of Cadleigh Property. Times (London), June 12, 1891, page 16.

The land was sold and then re-sold in 1892 and 1907, and again in 1910. In 1950 it was purchased by the Coldwell family who owned it until 1972. Sharon and Stephen Murphy have owned the property for many years and operate the Cadleigh Manor Bed & Breakfast.

Cadleigh House, as it looked in 1950. Photo courtesy of Sharon and Stephen Murphy.

Elizabeth Metherel Lethbridge died on September 14, 1859. Her husband, Thomas Lethbridge, died on January 11, 1861. Thomas left an estate of just under 2,000 British pounds[32]. Their gravestones stand in St. Peter and St. Paul Church Burial Ground, Ermington.

Many ancestral tombstones can be found among those in the lovely churchyard of St. Peter and St. Paul Church, Ermington. Some names are combined on the same stone while others stand alone. Memorials to children who passed away provide evidence of the high rate of infant mortality in Victorian England. Abbott markers are found next to those of the Lethbridges, Turpins, Metherels, etc. Upon visiting, one is somehow comforted by seeing them grouped together. These families remained close to their place of origin. Those who left were definitely the exceptions.

The author in the main floor suite at Cadleigh Manor. The room may have served as a parlour for the Lethbridge Family. Photo courtesy of Joseph Romain.

Entrance to the churchyard of St. Peter and St. Paul Church in Ermington, Devon. Photo courtesy of the author.

Lethbridge tombstones, Ermington, Devon. Photo courtesy of the author.

Abbott tombstone, St. Peter and St. Paul's Churchyard, Ermington. Photo courtesy of the author.

    William Abbott and Lydia Lethbridge were born within two miles of each other and within two years of each other. They were second cousins because their grandparents were siblings. They would have attended the same schools and churches and been part of the same non-parochial community. They would have encountered each other frequently in the Village of Lee Mill Bridge as the inn was a social centre and the forge was essential for the manufacture of tools and implements used on the farm. Cadleigh, Woodland, Ugborough, Ermington, Yealmpton were all within easy walking distance of the main Plymouth Road that linked their farms and villages in South Devon. William and Lydia were married on November 15, 1854, in St. Peter and St. Paul Church, Ermington[33]. Their sisters, Laura Lethbridge and Miriam Abbott witnessed their marriage.

William Abbott and Lydia Lethbridge were married in this church. St. Peter and St. Paul's Church, Ermington, Devon, interior.

William and Lydia's marriage registration. General Registry Office. Marriage, 1854.

In Devonshire

EMIGRATION

The population of Ermington Parish was growing as William and Lydia were making their decision to emigrate. In 1870-72, John Marius Wilson's *Imperial Gazetteer of England and Wales* described Ermington in these words:

> **ERMINGTON**, a village, a parish, and a hundred in Devon. The village stands on a bold eminence, contiguous to the river Erme, 2 miles NW of Modbury, and 2¾ S of Ivy-bridge r. station; was formerly a place of some importance, with a weekly market; and has a post office under Ivy-Bridge, and fairs on 2 Feb. and 24 June. The parish [Ermington] also includes part of Ivy-bridge; and is in Plympton-St. Mary district. Acres, 4, 952. Real property, £9, 434. **Pop. in 1851, 1, 423; in 1861, 1, 785.** [**in 1871, 2,010**].[34]

One could be forgiven for wondering why William Abbott, the eldest son in his family, a skilled tradesman, a master blacksmith, at the age of thirty-nine, living in the bosom of his ancestral roots, would leave his home in Devon in 1871 and journey across the Atlantic to settle in the small town of Belmont in North Dorchester Township, Middlesex County with his pregnant forty year old wife Lydia and their eight children, two of whom were apprenticed in the same trade.

Why did he decide to emigrate? Was the relentless progress of the railway making the skills of the small scale smith redundant? Was the local economy of North Dorchester Township in the new Dominion of Canada too strong to resist? Where the reports of other Canadian immigrants just too compelling? Was William Abbott ambitious and intent on land ownership and prosperity despite the risks?

William and Lydia had seven sons and one daughter. It was assumed that their daughter would marry, but the seven sons all needed a trade. The rural economy of Southwest England experienced a slump between 1860 and 1880 due to strong competition from the United States whose rural economy increased by 100 per cent in these decades compared to a fifteen per cent decline in England. This affected the economy of Devon in particular whose wheat exports were outpaced by the flood of U.S. wheat on the European market[35]. Employment in the trades was difficult to find in the 1870s and land ownership was beyond the reach of most young men not born into the upper classes.

William was ambitious for himself and for his family. He was baptized and raised as a Wesleyan Methodist. Although there is no evidence to suggest that he was a particularly religious man, Methodists generally saw immigration as a great form of self-improvement, a way to improve one's lot in life in the eyes of God. This belief may have influenced his decision to emigrate.

William would also have read the letters of cousins and heard the reports from neighbours who had already emigrated from Devon to Ontario who had been able to purchase land a short while after settling in Ontario.

He would have been a keen observer of assisted passage schemes and would have applied for any assistance available to offset the costs of the ocean voyage with his large family.

Land ownership would provide the family with stability and status. William and Lydia were tenants in Devon. They rented or leased their land and saw no reasonable prospect of becoming landowners there. The 1870s saw a substantial increase in immigration to Canada as both rural and city dwellers saw opportunities to acquire land that simply did not exist in Britain.[36] Although the period of study is a few decades earlier, William Wylie in *The Blacksmith in Upper Canada, 1784-1850* [37] says that "Land was valued so highly, both in economic and cultural terms that the trades had become stepping stones to land ownership. Also, newspaper advertisements indicate that apprentices were in great demand in Upper Canada as a source of affordable labour".

An advertisement by Government of Canada to promote assisted passage to Canada. Library and Archives Canada, C-63484.

Chapter 3
The Immigrants

In mid-June of 1871, William and Lydia Abbott and their large family travelled from rural Devon to Liverpool. On June 16, 1871, they embarked on board the *S.S. Prussian,* a steamship operated by the Montreal Ocean Steamship Company. The ship was bound for Quebec via Londonderry. After 10 long days at sea, the Abbotts landed in Quebec City on the 26th of June, 1871.

S.S. Prussian steamship of the Allan Line circa, 1869-1898. Library and Archives Canada, C-067378.

The *S.S. Prussian* was built in 1869. Weighing 2,794 tons, it was one of the smaller steamships of the Allan Line whose fleet ranged between 1,101 and 18,481 tons. It had a capacity of 700 adult passengers. An association of steamship companies, known as The North Atlantic Conference, had consistently maintained the steerage or immigrant fare for an adult on steamships at 6 British Pounds and 6 Shillings. While this agreement ceased in 1875, it would have been in place when the Abbotts were emigrating in 1871. [38] If we assume that the Abbotts travelled by steerage, one estimate of the current value of the fare for two adults would have been about $1250.18 in 2019 U.S. Dollars, (based on one British Pound being equal to five U.S. Dollars in 1880).[39] The cost for 2 adults in 2019 US dollars would have been about $1250.18. There were also eight children's fares, so this was indeed a substantial investment in their future.

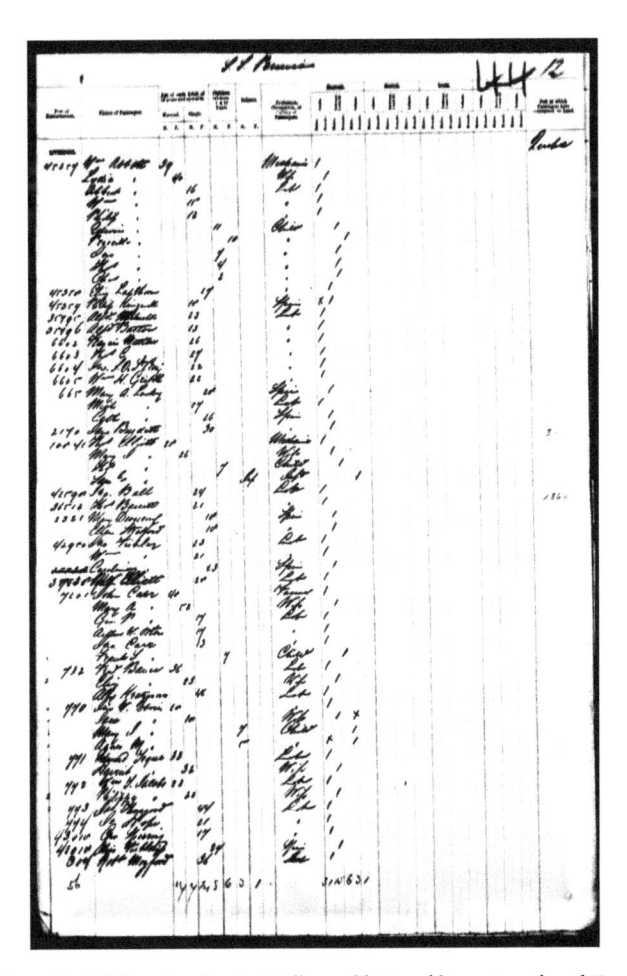

Ship's manifest of the S.S. Prussian showing William Abbott and his party on board. Passenger Lists: Quebec Arrivals, 1865-1935. Passenger List: Priscilla Abbott© Government of Canada. Reproduced with the permission of Library and Archives Canada (2019). Source: Library and Archives Canada/RG76-C-1-a, item number 202152

A copy of the ship's manifest shows the entry for the Abbott family.[40] Lydia was forty years old, William was thirty-nine. William's occupation was stated as "Mechanic". The children ranged in age from Albert who was sixteen to Charles who was two years old. The family was accompanied by Miss Elizabeth Lapthorne, age seventeen, and Mr Philip Kingwell, age eighteen. Kingwell was William Abbott's nephew and Miss Lapthorne may have assisted Lydia Abbott with her large family.

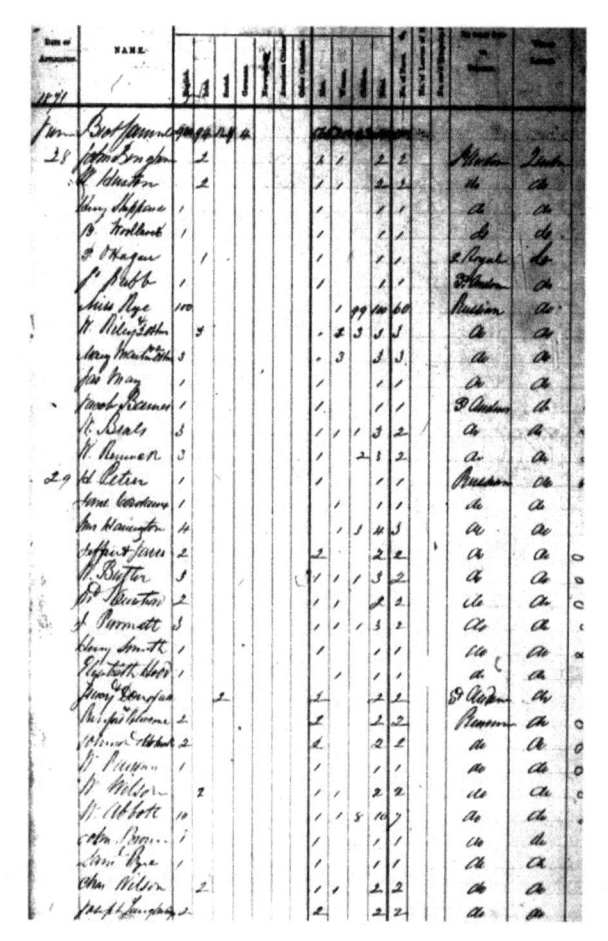

Assisted Immigration Register showing William Abbott and family.
Toronto Emigration Office assisted immigration register, William Abbott,
1871, RG 11-3, vol. 2, Archives of Ontario

We can document one of the first references to the Abbott family's arrival in Canada from an application for assistance they made at the *Toronto Emigrant Office*.[41] The Archives of Ontario provides some background about this office and the service it provided to immigrants in the province: "The primary function of the Emigrant Office was to assist newly-arrived immigrants by providing provisions and temporary shelter, and by helping them to find medical care, employment, and transportation to their final destination"[42].

Records of the Emigrant Office agent A.B. Hawke, document the application on June 29, 1871, of an Englishman, W. Abbott, who was part of a party of two adults and eight children, who had travelled on board the ship, *The Prussian*. We can see the entry for W. Abbott on the fifth line from the bottom of the Assisted Immigration Register.

Once they had disembarked, it is not known for certain just how the Abbotts travelled from Quebec City to Toronto. A likely route would have been by the *Grand Trunk Railway* and *Great Western Railway* which had extensive networks of lines by 1871. The Abbotts might have boarded a train in Quebec City, travelled as far as Toronto, where we know they stopped at the *Toronto Emigrant Office*. The *Great Western Railway* station occupied the south-east corner of Yonge and Front Street where the Sony Centre (formerly O'Keefe Centre) is today. They might have then boarded a Great Western train to Hamilton and from there travelled on toward London. Another possibility is a trip by steamer on the St. Lawrence River and Lake Ontario to Toronto, then by train to Dorchester or London.

Great Western Railway Station Toronto, 1867 showing south-east corner of Yonge and Front Streets, Toronto. This station may have been used by the Abbotts when they transferred from the Grand Trunk Railway Line travelling from Quebec City in 1871.

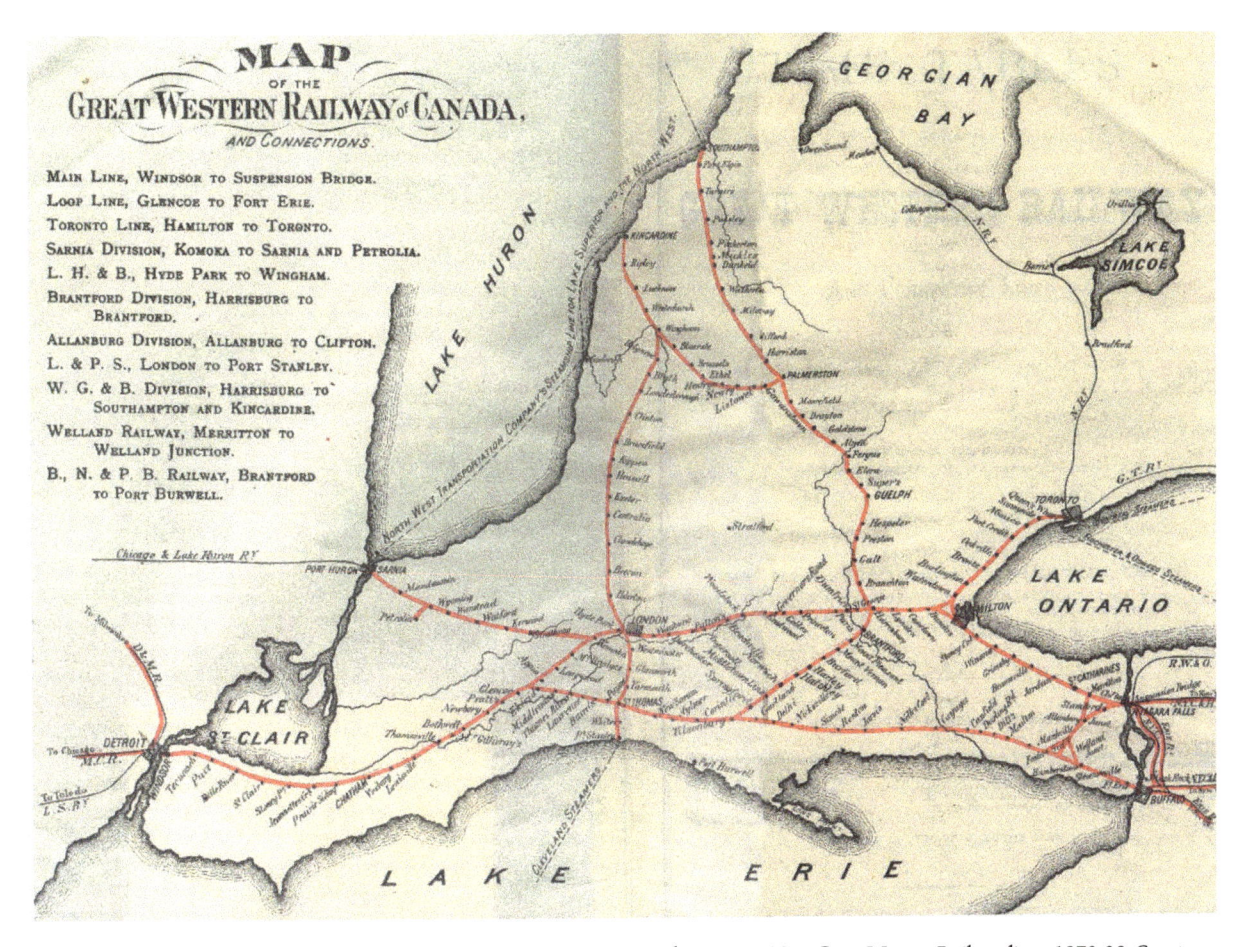

Railway routes across Southwestern Ontario in the 1870s. Great Western Railway Route Map. Great Western Railway lines, 1879-80. Courtesy of http://www.trainweb.org/oldtimetrains/CNR/gwr/history.htm

There were several railway stations in Elgin and Middlesex Counties by the 1870s. The Abbotts may have travelled to any of the nearby stations at London, Westminster, Glanworth, or Dorchester, or they may have travelled to London, arriving in Belmont after several hours by wagon or horse-drawn coach. They, no doubt, felt excitement and some trepidation arriving in a strange new place, after the long overland journey and many difficult days at sea.

BELMONT, ONTARIO

By 1871 the village of Belmont had a post office, school, a harness maker's shop, a blacksmith forge and a handful of stores selling general goods. According to a paper given by Mrs George of the Women's Institute in 1932, a post office had been established in the 1830s at the corner of the 6th concession of North Dorchester. At that time the settlement was called "Plymouth". The mail had been delivered by a Mr Prouse, a native of Plymouth, England who had named the site of the post office after his home town in England. As the blacksmith and the harness maker shops were established and the settlement began to grow, it took the name "Belmont".[43] By 1875 with a population of 500, Belmont was a prosperous village at the intersection of four townships in two large counties: Elgin and Middlesex.

William and Lydia Abbott would have been aware of the Belmont area from many families from Devon who had immigrated to the area before them. They may also have chosen Belmont as a place to settle because William and his sons had the iron-smithing skills that were in demand in the burgeoning farm community.

Fonds in the collection of the Elgin County Archives contain first-hand accounts of life in early Belmont. One description states, "The Village of Belmont was first surveyed in 1851 and two years later the [Belmont] Post Office was established. In the following years, Belmont thrived and a good number of businesses were established, such as saw and grist mills, a cheese factory, carriage works and harness shops... [However] When the Credit Valley Railway was built in 1881, it ruined business for the village as it became easier to travel to St. Thomas"[44]. This observation reflects the Abbott's fortunes. Having arrived in Belmont in 1871, William and Lydia had done their homework, assuming that the growing village would continue to thrive and make a successful location for William's blacksmith business. However, perhaps the village economy couldn't support the established forges and the numerous trained blacksmiths in the Abbott family. Within six years William had purchased land at Concession 6, Lot 18, near Gladstone, and turned his hand to farming.

Tragically, the earliest official documentation of the Abbotts settling in North Dorchester Township was the registration of the death of Lydia less than six months after their arrival in Ontario. On January 11, 1872, Lydia died in childbirth after four days confinement. Although the infant has been referred to as "Baby Lydie" in family lore, I have found no registration of the birth or stillbirth of the child.

Lydia Lethbridge Abbott (1831-1872), c. 1870, prior to emigration from Devon. Photograph taken by J. Grey, Photographer, Stonehouse, Devon. Courtesy of North Dorchester Heritage Book Committee.

No nineteenth-century tombstone for Lydia has ever been located. However, in May 2010 an experienced dowser, Mae Leonard from Otterville, Ont., examined the burial plot of William Abbott in the Dorchester Union Cemetery. She reported[45] that there is evidence that Lydia was buried to the right side of William Abbott. Lydia appears to have a child cradled in her left arm. Following their discussion of this report, descendants of Lydia raised the funds to have a grave marker made to mark her burial site. It was placed on the Abbott burial plot in 2013.

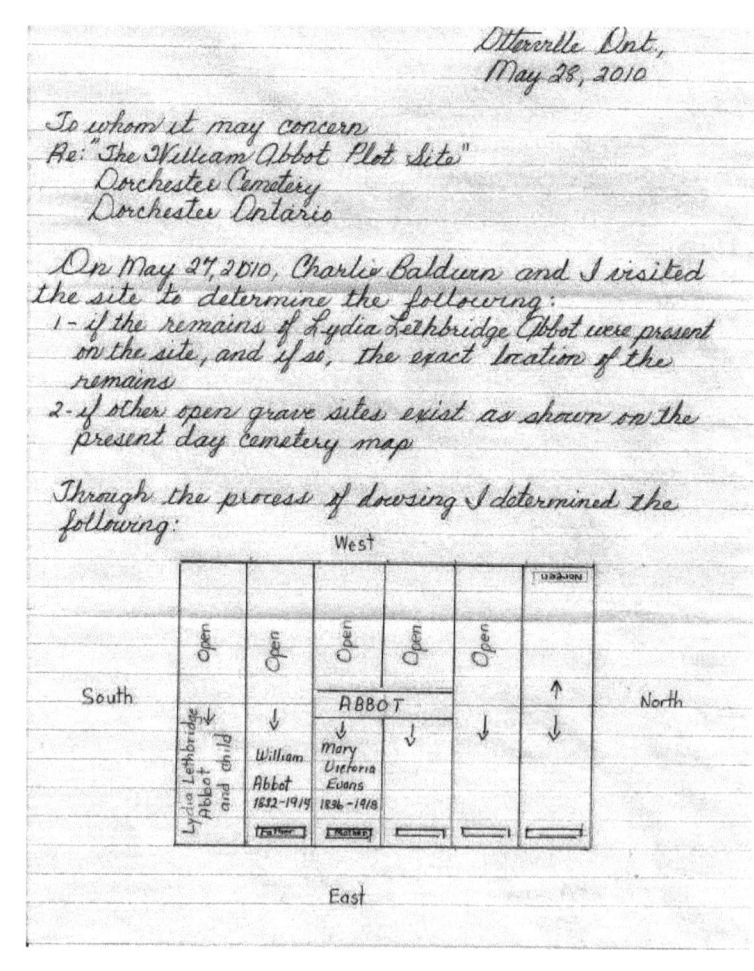

Mae Leonard dowsing report, first page of three. Sent to Charles Baldwin, 2010.

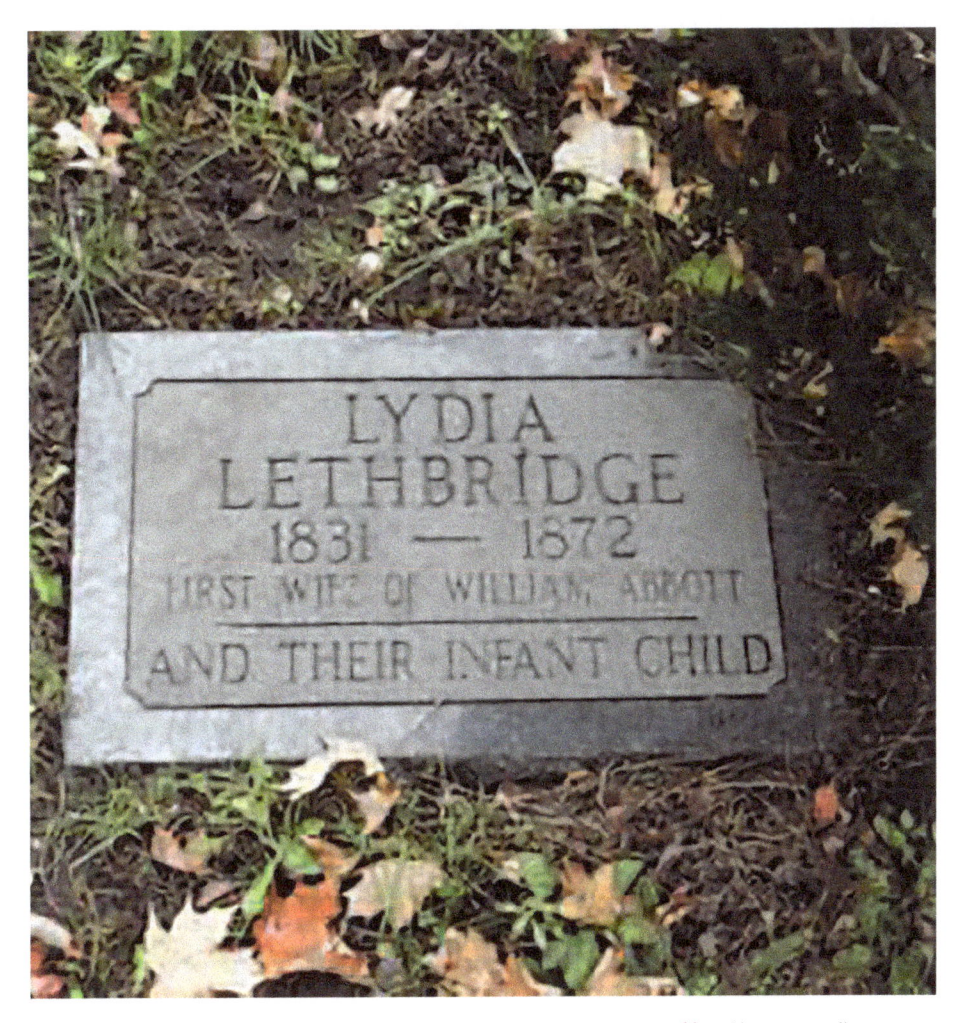

Lydia Lethbridge Abbott grave marker, Dorchester Union Cemetery. Sponsored by Abbott-Kingwell Reunion, made and installed by Dan Stewart, 2010-11. Photo courtesy of Janice Brain.

Lydia was forty-one years old when she died. Her husband, William, was left with eight grieving children, two of them under five years of age. Her death registration[46] states that she was a blacksmith's wife, born in Devonshire, England and that her husband William Abbott was a blacksmith in Belmont. He had been in Ontario for a little over six months and now he was a widower and his children needed a mother.

William soon met Mary Victoria Evans of Harrietsville. They were married in Belmont on January 7, 1873.[47] Mary was born on May 24, 1836, in New York State. She was the daughter of a John Evans (1805–1885) and Sarah Robinson Evans (1810–1887). The Evans had emigrated from England and settled in Mercer County, Pennsylvania.

Mary Victoria Evans, c.1856, taken in Ingersoll, Ontario. Photocopy of photo courtesy of Dorothy Garton.

Mary Victoria Evans was one of seven children. Her eldest brother, Thomas, was born in England in about 1832. Mary was born in New York State in 1836, perhaps just as the family arrived from England. Then the Evans moved to Pennsylvania where Sarah (1839-1877), James (1840-), John (1844-), Charlotte (1848-), and Martha (1850-) were born[48]. Her youngest sister Martha was a witness at Mary's marriage to William Abbott.

The entry for Mary in the 1901 Census of Canada indicated that she immigrated to Canada in 1857.[49] Indeed, we find her living with her parents and siblings in 1861 in Yarmouth Township, Elgin County[50]. By the time the 1871 enumeration was taken, Mary *Ann* [sic] was living in North Dorchester, Middlesex County.

When she married in 1873 she was thirty-seven years old and was taking on a huge amount of work and responsibility in raising the eight Abbott children.

William and Mary Abbott, c. 1900. Photo courtesy of Mary E. Abbott collection.

William and Mary's son Alfred was born on October 28, 1873. The family lived in Belmont for six years. Directories for North Dorchester for 1874 and 1875 list William Abbott as occupying Concession 6 Lot 24 in Belmont.

The Immigrants

On October 29, 1877, William and Mary Abbott bought land from John Dennis on the Sixth Concession, Lot 18, North Dorchester, just south of the village of Gladstone. They paid $6,100.00 for one hundred acres which comprised the north half and part of the south half of the lot[51]. Calculations don't currently go back as far as 1877, but if this amount were paid in 1914, its value in today's Canadian Dollars would be $135,741.00.[52]

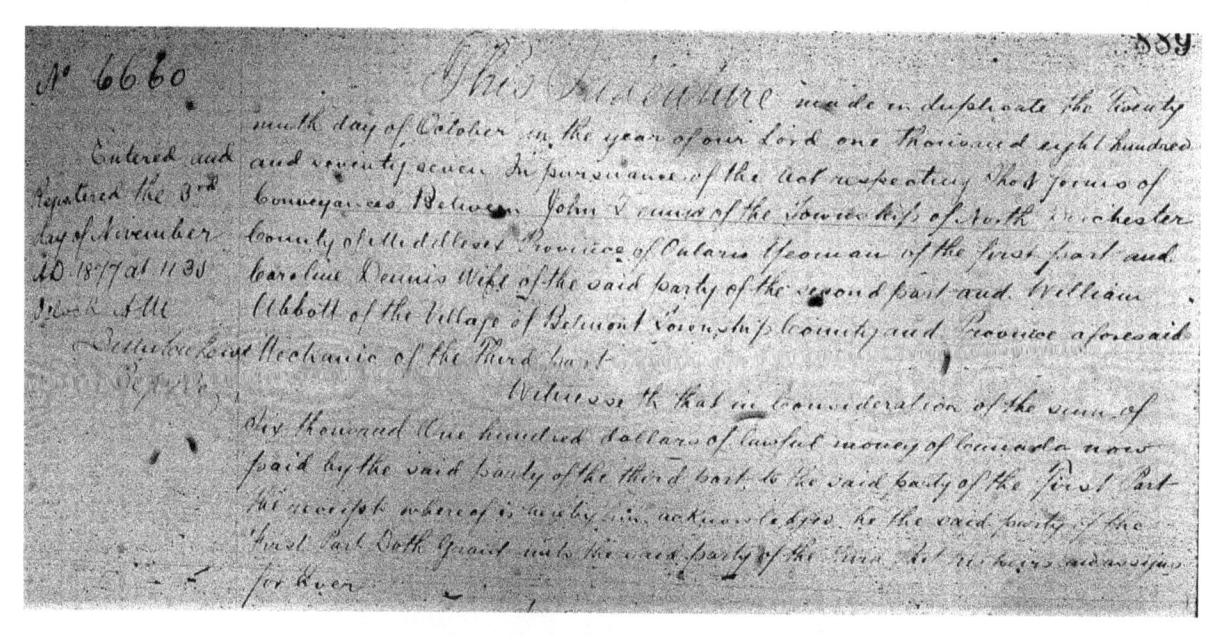

The deed to the property on Concession 6, Lot 18, North Dorchester Township, 1877. Archives of Ontario/ RG 53-55/ Middlesex County Land Registry. Instruments and Deeds, 1877, No. 6660, Pg. 889/ Copyright Public Domain

The Abbotts bought the remaining portion of the south half from John Dennis at the same time with Dennis holding the mortgage of $3,100.00 which was discharged by 1881.

The Canadian County Atlas Digital Project undertaken by McGill University is a searchable database of the property owners' names which appear on the township maps in the nineteenth-century county atlases. Township maps, portraits and properties have been scanned, with links from the property owners' names in the database. The Historical Atlas of the County of Middlesex illustrates the Township of North Dorchester and its lots and concessions. The north half of Concession 6, Lot 18 contains the name of "Wm. Abbott". There is a farmhouse illustrated in the north-west corner of the lot just west of Harrietsville.[53]

Map of part of North Dorchester Township showing the Abbott property. Canadian County Atlas Digital Project, Middlesex County (Ontario Map Ref #5), Illustrated historical atlas of the county of Middlesex, Ont. Toronto: H.R. Page & Co., 1878. Courtesy of Rare Books and Special Collections, McGill University Library.

William's granddaughter, Mary E. Abbott, the daughter of Charles and Sara Abbott, wrote in her family research that the Abbotts lived in Belmont for five years and operated a blacksmith's shop. Directories of 1874 and 1875 indicate that William Abbott resided in Belmont on Concession 6, Lot 24. After purchasing the farm at Concession 6, Lot 18 in 1877, the family settled into rural ways and ventured into farming. The hamlet of Gladstone would have been their closest community. Gladstone had a post office (opened in 1864), a blacksmith shop, a general store, a woodworking shop and a cider mill and by the 1880s a railway line and cheese factory. The Abbott children of school age would have attended Gladstone School.

In the 1881 Ontario Census William was enumerated as a farmer, living with his wife, Mary and all their children except Albert & William Jr. who had left the family home to start businesses and homes of their own.[54] Lovell's Directory of 1882 places William Abbott Sr. in Gladstone and Albert Abbott as Glanworth's blacksmith. William Abbott Jr. was listed as a wagon maker in Belmont in the same directory. By 1883 the

The Immigrants

North Dorchester directory lists William Abbott Sr. as occupying Concession 6, Lot 18 in Harrietsville, while William Jr. was living on the same Belmont Concession 6, Lot 24 where the family lived when they first settled in Belmont in 1871.

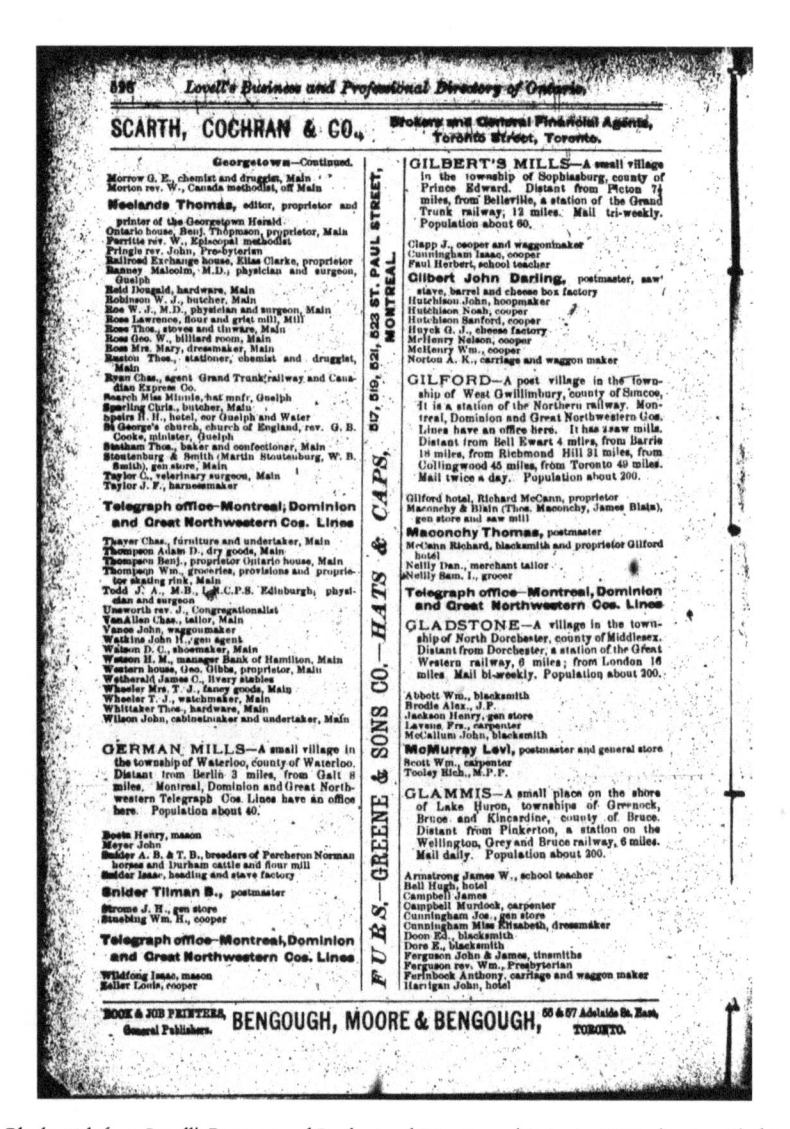

Wm. Abbott, Blacksmith from Lovell's Business and Professional Directory of Ontario, 1882, showing Gladstone businesses.

Abbott family in 1881. Census of Canada, 1881, Middlesex East, Dist. 167, Sub. Dist. Dorchester North B2, Page 17, Household 91. Library and Archives Canada. Census of Canada, 1881: Abbot, William © Government of Canada. Reproduced with the permission of Library and Archives Canada (2019). Source: Library and Archives Canada/RG31, item number 4278238

The 1891 Ontario Census entry for William and Mary shows the family farming with sons Charles and Fred at home. In addition, a thirteen-year-old wage earner, named William Burrell, lived with them. There are no other Burrells in Middlesex or Elgin county Census indexes, and according to the 1891 Census, William was born in England to Scottish parents. He may well have been one of the over 100,000 "Home Children" brought to Canada from England to work as agricultural labourers between 1869 and the 1930s.[55]

The Immigrants

In February of 1893, William and Mary took a mortgage on the property from Archibald and John Taylor. The mortgage may have been to finance the construction of a new house which still stands on the property. This mortgage was discharged in 1900.[56]

There were two houses on Concession 6, Lot 18 by 1897. The house on the north-west corner was the original farmhouse which was occupied by William and Mary and their children until 1897 when the new house was constructed. A photo of the cornerstone indicates the date it was placed during construction by Mrs Abbott.

Cornerstone of Abbott/Shackleton House, Concession 6, Lot 18, North Dorchester. Courtesy of Janet Rigsby, 2017.

The Abbott house was a solid yellow brick two-story farmhouse built to accommodate a large family. It was designed in the British Military style with a four-sided pyramidal roof. The front veranda had a gingerbread-style fascia and there was a stained glass transom in the front window that served to soften the plain appearance of the house. It had an east-west orientation with a north-south wing on the west side that accommodated a second staircase which lead to the bedrooms and indoor washroom on the second floor. A double parlour and dining room framed the central hall. The building project was ambitious when it was constructed in 1897 as only two of the Abbott's nine children remained at home at the time. The Abbott's may have been planning for their son Fred's future, and indeed Fred and Elizabeth Abbott and their children lived in the house until 1918 when they sold to Lorne Shackleton.

Abbott/Shackleton House, c. 1918. Shackleton children, left to right: Clayton, Dorothy, Alma, Hazel, and either Donald or Harry Shackleton. Photo Margaret Abbott Shackleton's photo collection.

Abbott/Shackleton House, rear view, c. 1935. Photo Margaret Abbott Shackleton's photo collection.

In 1901 the Ontario Census shows William, Mary and Frederick (sic) in addition there are two unrelated young people employed by the family, a domestic servant, Lillie Archer age sixteen, and a farm worker, nineteen-year-old Oliver Rolston.

By the time of the 1911 Census, William and Mary Albott (sic) were initially enumerated at Concession 6 Lot 18 as a separate family in a separate household from their son Fred and his wife Elizabeth, but the Census was corrected by striking a line through the dwelling column, indicating that they shared a dwelling with Fred, age twenty-seven, and his wife Elizabeth and their two children. Fred and Elizabeth employed a twenty-five-year-old servant named Thomas Berry[57].

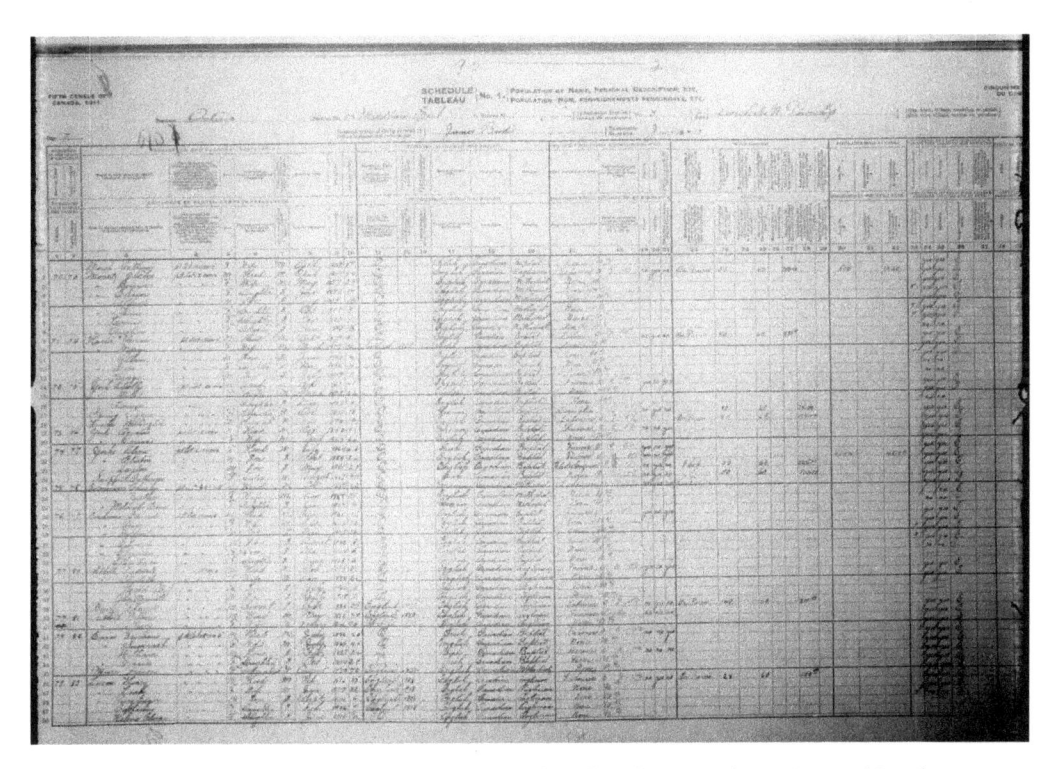

William and Mary Abbott, Fred and Elizabeth Abbott and family in the census of 1911. Census of Canada, 1911: Abbott, William © Government of Canada. Reproduced with the permission of Library and Archives Canada (2019). Source: Library and Archives Canada/RG31, item number 6225734

Fred purchased the farm property from William and Mary in May of 1911 except for one-half acre on the north-west corner which was retained by William and Mary. William and Mary held the mortgage of $8000.00. Was the Census correction due to the fact that there were still two separate dwellings on the lot at least until 1911 although two families shared one residence?

According to Mary E. Abbott, the daughter of William's son Charles, William made several visits back to Devon, England to visit family. "While living in Belmont he returned to England for a visit with relatives and was accompanied back to Canada by Isaac Kingwell". Isaac was the brother of Philip Kingwell who had accompanied the family when they first emigrated in 1871. "In 1899 William returned to England along with his son Albert and visited his mother for the last time."

The Immigrants

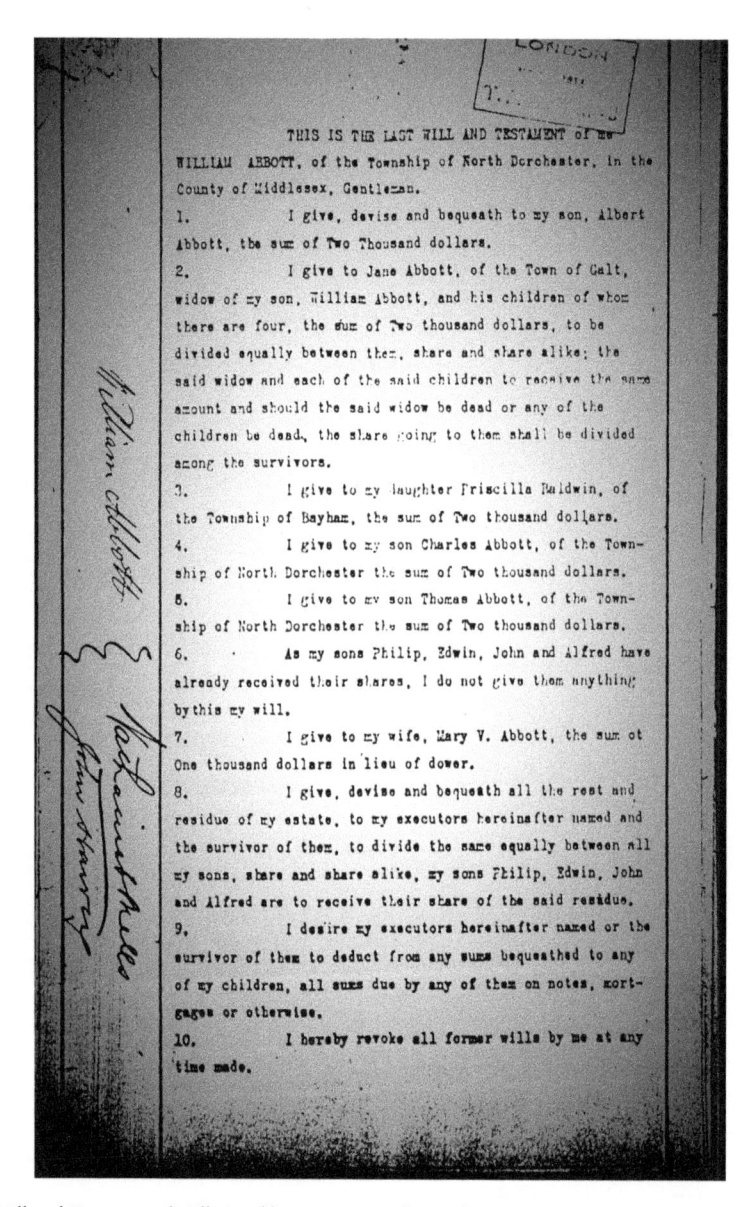

THIS IS THE LAST WILL AND TESTAMENT of me WILLIAM ABBOTT, of the Township of North Dorchester, in the County of Middlesex, Gentleman.

1. I give, devise and bequeath to my son, Albert Abbott, the sum of Two Thousand dollars.

2. I give to Jane Abbott, of the Town of Galt, widow of my son, William Abbott, and his children of whom there are four, the sum of Two thousand dollars, to be divided equally between them, share and share alike; the said widow and each of the said children to receive the same amount and should the said widow be dead or any of the children be dead, the share going to them shall be divided among the survivors.

3. I give to my daughter Priscilla Baldwin, of the Township of Bayham, the sum of Two thousand dollars.

4. I give to my son Charles Abbott, of the Township of North Dorchester the sum of Two thousand dollars.

5. I give to my son Thomas Abbott, of the Township of North Dorchester the sum of Two thousand dollars.

6. As my sons Philip, Edwin, John and Alfred have already received their shares, I do not give them anything by this my will.

7. I give to my wife, Mary V. Abbott, the sum of One thousand dollars in lieu of dower.

8. I give, devise and bequeath all the rest and residue of my estate, to my executors hereinafter named and the survivor of them, to divide the same equally between all my sons, share and share alike, my sons Philip, Edwin, John and Alfred are to receive their share of the said residue.

9. I desire my executors hereinafter named or the survivor of them to deduct from any sums bequeathed to any of my children, all sums due by any of them on notes, mortgages or otherwise.

10. I hereby revoke all former wills by me at any time made.

Last Will and Testament of William Abbott, page 1. Archives of Ontario/ RG 22-321/ Middlesex County. Estate File #11935, Estate of William Abbott, 1914-15/ Copyright Public Domain

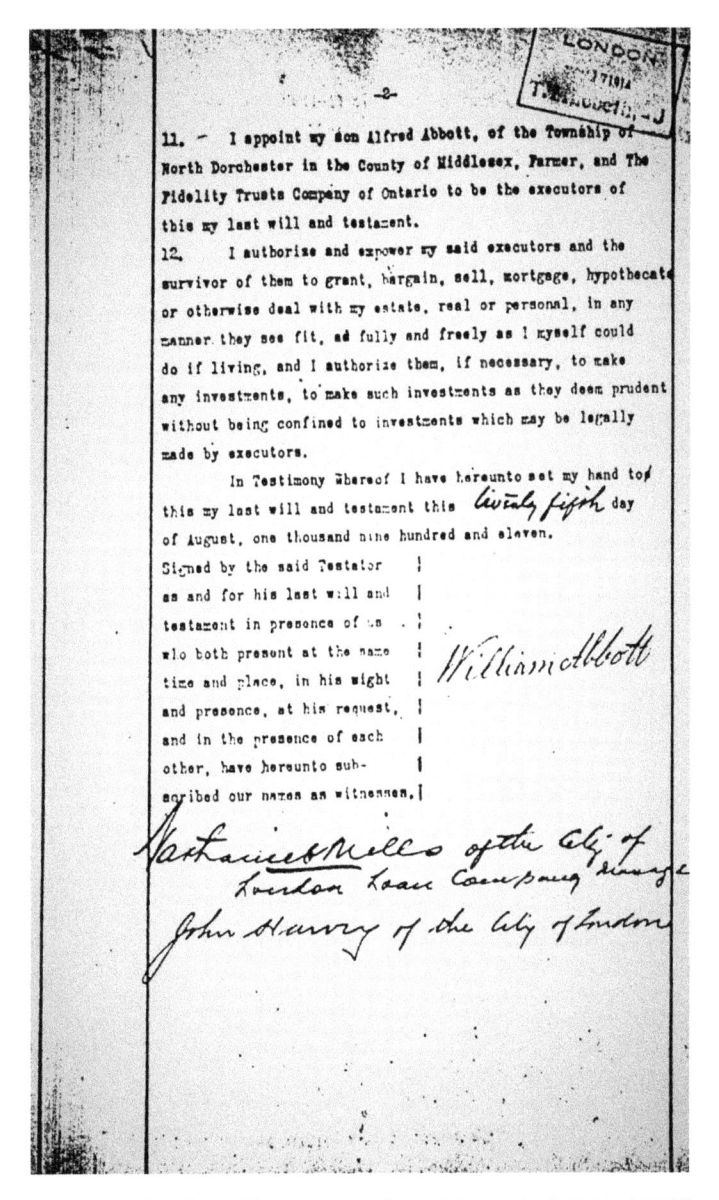

— 2 —

11. — I appoint my son Alfred Abbott, of the Township of North Dorchester in the County of Middlesex, Farmer, and The Fidelity Trusts Company of Ontario to be the executors of this my last will and testament.

12. I authorise and empower my said executors and the survivor of them to grant, bargain, sell, mortgage, hypothecate or otherwise deal with my estate, real or personal, in any manner they see fit, as fully and freely as I myself could do if living, and I authorize them, if necessary, to make any investments, to make such investments as they deem prudent without being confined to investments which may be legally made by executors.

In Testimony Whereof I have hereunto set my hand to this my last will and testament this *twenty fifth* day of August, one thousand nine hundred and eleven.

Signed by the said Testator as and for his last will and testament in presence of us who both present at the same time and place, in his sight and presence, at his request, and in the presence of each other, have hereunto subscribed our names as witnesses.

William Abbott

Nathaniel Mills of the City of London Loan Company Manager

John Harvey of the City of London

Last Will and Testament of William Abbott, page 2. Archives of Ontario/ RG 22-321/ Middlesex County. Estate File #11935, Estate of William Abbott, 1914-15/ Copyright Public Domain

The Immigrants

It has been said that William Abbott fell off a roof at the age of eighty-two, and indeed, his death registration confirms that William died as a result of a concussion suffered for three days before his death on October 16, 1914[58]. His death notice in the *London Free Press* mentions only his death date, his age, where he died, on the Gladstone farm, the date of his funeral, Oct. 19, 1914, and his burial in Dorchester Union Cemetery[59].

If we examine his will, we learn that William Abbott owned some pockets of real estate in Western Canada. He purchased two lots in Winnipeg, Manitoba and eight lots in Swift Current, Saskatchewan. William and Mary also purchased quarter acre properties on Lot 8 and Lot 9 on Catherine Street in Dorchester in 1912[60]. Several of his children had at one time or another received mortgages or loans.

His estate[61] was left to each of his surviving children and to the family of his predeceased son William Jr. Each child received the sum of $2000.00. In addition, one half acre of the Abbott farm on Concession 6, Lot 18 was left to his son Alfred, with the balance of his estate left in equal parts to each of his sons and to his wife, Mary. His daughter, Priscilla, was not included in the division of the balance of the estate.

The photograph below is from the collection of Charles Baldwin. It was among the photographs in an old album which was passed down to Charles Baldwin from his grandmother, Priscilla Abbott Baldwin. After the death of Priscilla's mother, Lydia, Mary Abbott raised eleven-year-old Priscilla. They were two women in a large household of men. There was bound to have been much solidarity and tenderness in that relationship.

Mary Victoria Abbott died a few years after her husband, William, on Oct. 29, 1918. She was eighty-two years old. Mary and William are buried in Dorchester Union Cemetery.

Tombstone of William and Mary Abbott, Dorchester Union Cemetery.

Mary Victoria Evans Abbott, c. 1910. Photo courtesy of Charles Baldwin.

Chapter 4
The Forerunners

William and Lydia Abbott were among the 30,000 immigrants who came to Canada in 1871. There was a massive amount of advertising aimed at the prospective immigrant, especially to those in Britain whose language and traditions were so compatible with those in the new Dominion. Immigrants' handbooks of the time offered advice to prospective immigrants. The Abbotts would read many such persuasive descriptions of the advantages offered to newcomers in Ontario and in the advertisements for Canadian immigration which appeared in British newspapers.

The following prospectus was extracted from Sessional Papers of the Province of Ontario, 1872[62].

> *The province of Ontario is situate to the North of the River St. Lawrence, and of the great lakes, Ontario, Erie, Huron, and Superior… No portion of the Dominion offers greater inducements to emigrants. What the country needs is men to clear the forest lands, to cultivate the soil, to build houses, to make the ordinary household goods, and to open up communication from one part of the country to another, by the construction of roads and railways. Of professional men, book-keepers, and clerks, Ontario has enough and to spare. Female household servants are always sure of immediate employment, at good wages. Dressmakers, milliners, and seamstresses can obtain much better wages than at home.*
>
> *Farmers of moderate means can purchase or lease farms more or less cleared and improved; and by discretion and industry, can scarcely fail to improve their condition, and to afford their children, as they grow up, a favourable start in life. Uncleared land is from 2shillings to 40shillings per acre. Improved farms can be bought at from £4 to £10 an acre. The money can nearly always be paid in instalments, covering several years... Emigrants possessing means*

should not be in a hurry to purchase, but get some experience before taking so important a step. Agricultural labourers would study their own interest by accepting employment as it may be offered, on arrival, and they will soon learn how to improve their condition.

Men commencing as labourers seldom keep in that condition very long, but after a brief period become employers of labour themselves. It is this moral certainty of rising in the social scale, that stimulates the exertions of the needy settler.

In Ontario, old country people will find themselves surrounded by comforts similar to those they left in the old land; religious privileges almost the same; and Public Free Schools established throughout the Province, which are attended by children of all classes.

Sterling Money and Canadian Currency: for general purposes, it will be sufficient to remember that the Canadian cent and the English half-penny are almost identical in value.

Wages in various trades:

Agricultural Labourers	*4 shillings to 6 shillings per day, without board.*
Agricultural Labourers	*50-80 shillings per month, with board.*
Carpenters	*6 shillings to 8 shillings per day.*
Bricklayers	*8 shillings to 10 shillings per day.*
Plasterers	*8 shillings to 10 shillings per day.*
Stone masons	*12 shillings to 14 shillings per day.*
Blacksmiths	**6 shillings to 9 shillings per day.**
Wheelwrights	*6 shillings to 9 shillings per day.*
Tailors piece-work	*at good wages.*
Shoemakers piece-work	*at good wages.*
Female servants general	*20 shillings to 32 shillings per month.*
Cooks	*28 shillings to 40 shillings per month.*

The Forerunners

Passage from Britain to Canada: All necessary information as to passage can be obtained of W. Dixon, Emigration Agent, 11 Adam Street, Adelphi, London; ... and of any other Canadian Emigration; and also of the Officers of Emigration Societies, or of the numerous Shipping Brokers in the United Kingdom.

Assisted Passages: The Government of Ontario will pay to regularly organized Emigration Societies in the United Kingdom or in Ontario, or to individuals, the sum of six dollars (£1 4s. 8s.) for every statute adult sent to this Province, at the end of three months' continuous residence in the Province....[63]

These facts would certainly be encouraging to those considering immigration, however, it is difficult to imagine a large family, with very young children, contemplating such a journey and permanent relocation without the recommendation of trusted relatives and friends who had immigrated successfully. Communication back to Devon from immigrants who had come and settled earlier would have been important. When the Abbotts were making their decision to emigrate, they had neighbours from Devon who were already settled and prospering.

Lydia Lethbridge Abbott's first cousin, Garland Lethbridge (1830-1899), left Devon and settled in North Dorchester with his wife Mary Ann and their seven children in 1870. They were enumerated in the 1871 Census of Ontario[64]. Their infant son, Christopher, was born in Ontario following their arrival. They later settled in Raleigh Township in Kent County, roughly sixty miles west of North Dorchester Township. Garland and Lydia's fathers, Thomas (1796-1861) and Christopher (1802-1865), were brothers.

Another cousin of Lydia's, Ann Lethbridge (1815-1889), immigrated with her husband, James Hele Rowse, and their children to North Dorchester in 1855. A son, John Lethbridge Rowse, married into the Venning Family, ultimately farming on Concession 2, Lot 10[65].

William Abbott's son John (Jack) Rowse Abbott was named for his paternal grandmother Priscilla Rowse. He came to Canada when he was a mere lad of eight years, but eventually, Jack would marry Annie Lapthorne the daughter of John Lapthorne and Mary Luxton Lapthorne. Annie's father, John Lapthorne, was a butcher in London, Ont. In 1857 his family had emigrated from Devon to Ontario. In Devon, they had been neighbours of the Abbotts and the Lethbridges in Yealmpton. When John Lapthorne was enumerated in Yealmpton in 1851[66] he was working as a farm labourer on a local farm. When the Abbotts emigrated in 1871 they were accompanied by Elizabeth Lapthorne. She may have been a sister of John Lapthorne.

The 1878 Historical Atlas of the County of Middlesex shows many Abbott and Lethbridge names among the landowners who were cited on the detailed township maps[67].

In the Middlesex township of Ekfrid, Thomas, George, John and James Lethbridge owned property within about twenty-five miles of each other. The Ontario marriage records indicate that three of the four men were related, each having parents by the name of William and Mary Lethbridge of Devon, England. In addition to being related to each other, they are probably related to Lydia Lethbridge as they lived in adjacent south-east Devon parishes, at roughly the same time. The distance is about five miles and a walk of fewer than two hours from one place to the other. Lydia and William Abbott would have known these men and their families and this knowledge would have influenced their choice of where to settle in Ontario.

In Biddulph Township there were several men named Abbott who lived near the village of Lucan where Thomas Abbott's future wife Sarah Deacon was raised. It is likely that Thomas met Sarah through contact with other Abbotts in the area.

When William Abbott died in 1914 many of his children had settled in the surrounding area of North Dorchester Township, some eventually moving to the nearby City of London, Ontario. In time, the next generation would spread more broadly across Southwestern Ontario, throughout Southern Manitoba and into the Lake Ontario communities of Hamilton and Toronto, and further still, across the border into Michigan and beyond.

Family bonds were strong within this family. The First Annual Abbott Picnic in 1911 brought some of the family together. The Abbott-Kingwell Reunion continued the tradition through the following decades. Those who remained near Gladstone, Ontario would have done business with each other, helped each other in times of need and gathered for occasional visits. As children, many remember having Cousins in their school classes and meeting up with Aunts and Uncles on visits to town. Others, whose ancestors had left the Belmont area, would develop ties within their own branch of the family and would know little of their more distant relatives. The following chapters explore the descendant lines of each of William Abbott's children.

Chapter 5
Albert Abbott (1855-1929)

Albert Abbott was the eldest child of William and Lydia Abbott. Born on February 8, 1855, he was six years old and in school in Ermington, Devon when the 1861 Census of England was taken. By 1871 he was sixteen years old and working as a blacksmith, presumably as an apprentice at a nearby forge. Albert was described as a labourer, aged sixteen, on the Ship's Passenger List when he emigrated with the family and began a new life in Canada.

On March 19, 1879, at the age of twenty-four, Albert married Mary Page Parker (1854-1927) in North Dorchester. According to the marriage register, Albert was living in Glanworth, working as a blacksmith. Mary was the daughter of Alexander Edward Parker and Mary Anne Hortop Parker. According to the 1861 Census of Canada West, Alexander Parker was a miller. The Parkers lived in a log home in London Township with their five children. Mary was seven years old when the Census was taken[68]. There is evidence that the Parkers were married in Plymouth Devon[69].

Albert Abbott, Blacksmith from Lovell's Business and Professional Directory of Ontario, 1882, showing Glanworth businesses.

In 1880 Albert and Mary's daughter Evelyn Lydia (Eva) was born in Glanworth. A son, Maurice John, followed in 1884 by which time they had relocated to Belmont. A second daughter, Mary Pearl, was born in Belmont in 1888. By 1892 the family had moved to Thorndale where their fourth child, Gladys Emma, was born.

Albert Abbott and family, c. 1897. Seated: Mary Page Parker Abbott, Gladys Emma, Mary Pearl and Albert Abbott. Standing: Maurice John, Evelyn Lydia. Photo courtesy of North Dorchester Heritage Book Committee.

Directories of the period show Albert established in Glanworth in 1881 and 1883 as a freeholder on Concession 7, Lot 15 in Westminster Twp. Later he appears in the directories for Belmont in 1891 and Thorndale in 1894.

In the 1901 Census of Canada Albert and Mary were farming on Concession 3, Lot 2 West Nissouri Township (near Thorndale) along with their four children. They also had a boarder named Albert Baker who was a hired farm labourer[70]. They remained on the farm throughout 1911. The family attended Crumlin United Church.

Although I have found no documentation, some of their descendants recall that between 1911 and 1921 the family may have lived in the old industrial suburb of Pottersburg, Ontario. Annexed to the City of London in 1912, the area had been home to several potteries and had a post office and blacksmith shop which may have provided some occasional employment for Albert[71].

The will of William Abbott indicates that Albert and Mary were living at 43 Euclid Avenue in London. in 1914 when a list of family members was developed.[72] By 1921, the Census of Canada reveals that Albert and Mary had moved to 901 Queens Avenue, a property they owned in the east end of London. Albert was still listed as a blacksmith, but it's unlikely that he did much work at the age of sixty-seven. Only Mary Pearl and Evelyn remained at home as Gladys and Maurice had married[73].

Mary died in 1927 followed by Albert a few years later in 1929. Mary's death registration states that they lived at 906 (sic) Queens Ave. and had lived there since 1914[74]. Albert and Mary are both buried in Dorchester Union Cemetery alongside Evelyn.

Albert Abbott was remembered by his granddaughter, Erma Wilson Schuel, as having a broad moustache and it is said that when they finally settled in London, the family lived next door to the family of the popular bandleader Guy Lombardo, who was a London native and who was indeed born on Queen's Avenue in 1902.

Albert and Mary's daughter, Evelyn (Eva), had learning disabilities and did not attend school. She lived with her parents until their deaths and died at the age of fifty-five of stomach cancer in 1935. She lived at 240 Mount Pleasant Ave. in London and had been ill for several months before her death.

Maurice John was alternately called Morris, Morrie, and John Morris. At the age of thirty-three he married Elsie Fox in 1914. According to the 1921 Census they lived in London at 61 Beaconsfield Ave. They had three children, Donald Thomas who died as an infant (Dec. 20-23, 1916), M. (Maurice) Leslie, born May 11, 1918, and a third child, Beverly John, who is referenced in two family history charts[75], but I have found no documentary evidence of him. The Abbotts were living on Wortley Road in 1926 when Elsie died in November of an inflammation of the heart caused by a bacterial infection. Maurice later married Evelyn Bald in Oil Springs, Ontario on April 21, 1928. They were both merchants at the time of their marriage and later ran an upholstery, furniture and funeral parlour business in Oil Springs. M. Leslie Abbott died at the age of 41 on July 7, 1959. Maurice John and Evelyn both died in Sarnia in 1969 and are buried in Grandview Memorial Cemetery just outside of Sarnia, Ontario.

Mary Pearl was born in 1888 in Belmont. The 1921 Census indicates that she was a dressmaker before her marriage to William Talbot in 1923. They had a farm in Oil Springs and later sold it, moved to Mount Brydges and ran a grocery store for many years. Their children were Evelyn, William and Harold. Evelyn Talbot was born in 1924. She married James Lambert McCracken in 1945. They farmed the McCracken Family farm near Melbourne, Ontario. They had two children Rick and Sally. Evelyn moved to a nursing home before her death in 2010. Husband James lived his entire life in the farmhouse and continued farming until a year before his death in 2009 when he joined Evelyn in the nursing home. William Talbot was born in Mount Brydges, Ontario. He was only fourteen years old when his parents died. To enlist during World War II he had to exaggerate his age. After the war, he worked at Simpson's department store in London and later became a salesman for Samsonite luggage manufacturers. Bill married Muriel Moffat and they raised their children Wendy, Mary Jane and Bill in London. As retirement approached Bill and Muriel moved to Niagara-on-the-Lake. Bill died in 2013. Harold Talbot married Beatrice Brinklow Fishback. They lived in St. Thomas. Beatrice and Harold had Glenda, Ruby, Jim, Jeffrey, and Denny. Beatrice died in 2013.

Albert and Mary's youngest child, Gladys Emma, grew up in London, Ontario where she met Bertrand Wilson. She taught English at a Hebrew School in London for many years. Bertrand and Gladys married in 1919 and moved to Windsor, then later back to London. Their son, Glen Albert, was born in 1921, followed by a daughter, Erma Marilynn in 1925. Erma married Robert Schuel in Windsor and remained there until moving to Lindsay in retirement. Erma and Robert had a daughter Joanne and two sons, Robert and Douglas. Glen Albert Wilson married Barbara and settled in Toronto where he worked for General Electric.

Albert Abbott (1855-1929)

Chapter 6
William Abbott Jr. (1856-1887)

William Abbott Jr. was born on April 8, 1856, in Ermington Parish, near Ivybridge, Devon, England. When he was less than two months old, William was baptized in Plymouth at the Wesleyan Methodist Ebenezer Chapel[76]. He was five years old in the Census of 1861 Yealmpton, Plympton St. Mary Devon[77]. In the 1871 Census, William Jr. is not listed with the other members of his family. However, there is a William Abbott, age fourteen working as an agricultural servant on a neighbouring farm in the village of Lyneham. This could well be William Jr. as he was old enough to be working as a farm labourer.

William Jr. emigrated with the Abbott family in June of 1871. He was twenty years old and living in Belmont when he married Mary Jane Bratt (1854-1934) on March 14, 1877, in Westminster[78]. Mary Jane was the daughter of Samuel Oakley Bratt (1816-1885) and Mary Ann Cooper (1820-1911), both of Staffordshire England. Mary Jane was born on May 12, 1854, in Belmont. The Bratt family was well established in the County and owned acreage in Westminster Township. The 1878 Illustrated Historical Atlas of Middlesex County shows that Samuel Bratt owned three properties: two hundred acres in Concession 6, Lot 5; fifty acres in Concession 6, Lot 6; and twenty acres in Concession 5, Lot 5[79].

Four years after their marriage, William Jr. and Mary Jane had two young children Lillian, age three and Georgie, age one. William Jr. worked as a wagon maker and later a carriage maker. The family lived in Belmont among the families of other tradespeople including tailors, bakers, blacksmiths, cabinet makers, etc. The Census of 1881 provides an illustration of that village community[80].

William Abbott Jr and family living in Belmont in 1881. Census of Canada, 1881: Abbot, William © Government of Canada. Reproduced with the permission of Library and Archives Canada (2019). Source: Library and Archives Canada/RG31, item number 4278150

Commercial directories of the time indicate that William Abbott Jr. lived and worked in Belmont as one of three wagon makers in the village. The family lived on Concession 6, Part Lot 24. This is the same lot that William Abbott Sr. had purchased when he first appeared in the Belmont Directory in 1874. The property was purchased by William Abbott Sr. on August 21, 1872, and was later sold to William Jr. and his wife Mary Jane on October 9, 1877, although the deed was not registered until September 3, 1881[81].

Unfortunately, much of our understanding of William Jr. and Mary Jane Abbott's whereabouts between 1883 and 1892 depends on the accuracy of the London and Middlesex County directories of that time. Since the directories were a commercial resource and not an official record of who lived where at any given time, we can make assumptions about where people lived but they can't be relied upon with certainty. The directories show that the Abbotts occupied Westminster Township lots owned by Mary Jane's father Samuel Bratt. His twenty-acre property in Concession 5, Lot 5, Westminster was farmed by William Jr. and later by Mary Jane Abbott between 1887 and 1890[82] The Abbotts also farmed in Concession 6, Lot 5 in 1887[83].

William Jr. and Mary Jane Abbott had five children: three daughters – Lillian Blanche, Georgie Bratt, and Ada Clare and two sons – Stuart Stirling and Chester Cleveland.

Tragically, William Abbott Jr. died at the age of thirty-one on November 27, 1887, in Westminister Twp. Middlesex Co. He was buried on November 30, 1887, in Dorchester Union Cemetery. The cause of his death was pneumonia.

Although he died intestate, William Jr. and his wife Mary Jane were farming in Westminster and had retained Lots three and ten on the west side of College Street in Belmont. Mary Jane administered William Jr.'s estate and sold half of the property in Belmont in April of 1891 to William Mohr. She continued to hold one-fifth of an acre in Belmont. Mrs Abbott (Mary Jane) is listed as the freeholder in both Westminster and North Dorchester Townships[84].

Wm. Abbott Junr. Waggonmaker (sic), in Lovell's Business and Professional Directory of Ontario, 1882, showing Belmont businesses.

Mary Jane Abbott was a widow with five children by the time she was thirty-three years of age. Her youngest child Chester was four years old. She continued to farm in Westminster until at least 1891[85]. Her eldest son Stuart died of heart disease at the age of seven on May 31st 1892. This family had endured so much tragedy in just a few short years. By 1901 Mary Jane had moved to London. The 1901 Census shows that her daughter Lillian was a school teacher, while her daughter Ada Claire and son Chester Cleveland were both in school. Mary Jane's daughter, Georgie, was not enumerated with the family, perhaps she was attending Normal School working towards her teaching certification at the time.

By 1911 Mary Jane had moved to Galt, Ontario. She lived with Georgie who was, by then, a public school teacher.[86] Mary Jane Abbott eventually moved to Toronto where she lived at 91 Linsmore Crescent in East York until her death in 1934.

Ada Clare, Mary Jane and Georgie Abbott, circa 1910. Photo courtesy of Janice Brain.

William Abbott Jr. (1856-1887)

Mary Jane's eldest daughter, Lillian, married George Priddle, a schoolteacher. In 1921 they lived on Leslie St. in London.[87] Lillian and George lived on Ardaven Place in London in 1957 after George retired from teaching. Lillian died in 1963 and George in 1966. They had one son, William Welmore Priddle, born in 1904. William married Agatha Ryder in 1926 and they had five daughters: Nancy, Barbara, Elizabeth, Diane, and Susan.

Georgie Abbott was born on Dec 23, 1879. She became a teacher and worked in Galt and Hamilton. When Georgie retired she lived at 29 Compton Place, Hamilton[88]. She died on November 4, 1977, at the age of ninety-seven.

Ada was the third child of Mary Jane and William Abbott Jr. She was born on the 31st of October, 1882 in Belmont. She married John Charles Reading in London in 1907. They had three children: Dorothy, Douglas and Marjorie. Ada died at the age of forty-eight in 1931. John Charles Reading remarried Ellen Adeline Horning Dartnell, a widow, in Haileybury Ontario. They returned to live in Hamilton until John Charles' death in 1944. Dorothy Clare Reading married Barton Salmon of Muskoka Region and moved north to raise a family of three: Alan, Joyce (Joy) and Alyce-Jean. Alan Salmon married Helen Elliott. Joy Salmon Moon married Andrew Moon in 1964 and lived in Toronto, but moved back to Muskoka when Andrew died tragically. Alyce-Jean married Russell Thomas Ion. They had Jayne and Russell. Charles (Douglas) Reading married Margaret Howard. They raised their children in Hamilton until they moved to Milton in their later years. Douglas died on Jan. 31, 1997. They had three daughters: Clare, Brenda, and Claudia. Clare Reading married John James Lonnee in 1963. They had 4 children: Claudine, Mark, Chantelle and Matthew. Brenda Reading married Larry Clifford Brain in 1964. They had Howard and Lee. Claudia Reading married John Fredrick Stokes Donovan in 1970. There were two sons born: Patrick and Paul. Marjorie Eileen Reading was born in 1914 in Hamilton. She served as a Christian Missionary with the Prairie Bible Institute at Three Hills, Alberta and later in Fargo, North Dakota. She died of a brain tumor on July 1, 1994, in Minneapolis, Minnesota.

Information about William Jr. and Mary Jane Abbott's youngest child, Chester, is a somewhat contradictory. His United States draft card and application for exemption from January of 1917 state that he resided at 389 Third Street, Detroit with his wife (no name provided) and child (whose name was possibly Helen). He declared that he was employed as a driver by the National Express Company.[89] About a year later, on January

23rd, 1918 in London, Ontario, Chester joined the Canadian Expeditionary Force[90]. At that time he claimed he was single and living in Detroit at 161 Pitcher Street, working as a baker.

In the United States Census of 1940 Chester was an inmate of the Michigan State Penitentiary and Prison Farm. The census entry states Chester Cleveland, age fifty-two, married, born in Canada, with American citizenship[91]. Chester's sad story was related to me by his great-niece, Joy Moon. Apparently, he unwillingly became involved in a bar fight. The man he was fighting fell backwards, hit his head, and died of his injuries. Chester went to jail and served his sentence. He was called a model prisoner by jail officials, but when he was due to be released, he asked to remain in jail because he was afraid that the world had changed too much during his prison term[92]. Chester died in the Michigan State Penitentiary[93] on July 9, 1951, and was buried by the state.

Chapter 7
Philip Abbott (1858-1934)

Philip Abbott was the third son of Lydia and William Abbott. He was born in Ermington Parish, Devon on Nov. 24, 1858. Philip was twelve years old when the family immigrated to Canada. Philip married Sena Ann Baldwin on his twenty-seventh birthday, on Nov. 24, 1885, in Tillsonburg, Ontario. Sena grew up in Eden, Ontario. She was the eldest child of Samuel Baldwin and Abigail Ketchapaw and was born on September 29, 1861.

In 1881 Philip was the eldest son still living at home, farming with his father William. He married four years later. By 1891 Philip was married with three children and farming in North Dorchester, near his father and brothers. The Lovell directory of 1892 and 1894 lists Philip as a tenant farmer on Concession 5, Lot 12 in Harrietsville. Philip's brother Edwin was on Lot 16 and brother John was on Lot 20 in Gladstone, they are both listed as freeholders.

By 1901 Philip and Sena had a large family and farmed as tenants on a farm with the Strong Family near Orwell in Malahide Township. There is no evidence that Philip and Sena had ever been landowners. Perhaps they couldn't save enough to purchase a farm. I have heard that Sena had trouble getting along with some in the family. She may have resented that she lacked what others had.

Philip Abbott c. 1885. Charcoal drawing of Philip Abbott. Courtesy of Charles Baldwin.

Philip Abbott (1858-1934)

Philip and Sena Ann Abbott had eight children: Edwin Lewis (Lew) (1886-1956), Margaret (Maggie) May (1888-1949), Ellen Alzina (1890-1972), Ruby Abigail (1896-1974), Grace Agnes Mary (1898-1983), Alma Coral (1900-1989), Philip Henry Warren who died in infancy after only 4 days from March 23-27, 1902 in Malahide Twp., and their youngest child Lulu Loretta (1903-1971).

Sena Ann Baldwin and Philip Abbott, c. 1912. From Margaret Abbott Shackleton's photo album.

Sena kept a record of births, marriages and deaths in her family in a notebook, entitled *Mrs Abbott's Book*. She wrote a note to her granddaughter Dorothy Garton, dated July 1, 1933: "*I wish you health, I wish you wealth, I wish you heaven after death. What could I wish you more. Your grandmother, Mrs Philip Abbott.*" This would have been on a visit to Ontario in 1933, the year before Philip died in 1934. Sena died in 1947. They are both buried in Bethel Cemetery, in Treherne, Manitoba.

By 1906 Philip and Sena and their family lived in Glencolin with their son Lew. In 1911, Philip followed Lew and his wife, Sylvia, to Manitoba where they had settled about 120 kilometres southwest of Winnipeg, near the town of Treherne. Sena followed later with her three youngest children. The elder girls, Maggie, Ellen and Ruby remained in Ontario.

Their eldest child and only surviving son, Lew, was born on September 28, 1886. He married Sylvia Beatrice Anger on December 9 1908. The couple moved to Treherne, Manitoba the following year. Sylvia's brother, Harry Anger, had moved to Treherne earlier. Lew and Sylvia had three daughters: Beatrice, Lucille and Elva, all born in Manitoba. The 1911 Census shows that Lew, Sylvia and their daughter, baby Beatrice, lived together with Philip and Sena and their three daughters, Grace, Alma and Lulu. The 1916 Census for Manitoba, Saskatchewan and Alberta shows Lew and Sylvia living with their own three daughters in South Norfolk Township 8, Range 10 and Philip and Sena living nearby with their family in South Norfolk Township 8 Range 8.

Heartbreakingly, Sylvia died in childbirth on Nov. 22, 1918, and her baby boy died a few days later. Sylvia was buried in Bethel Cemetery, in Treherne, Manitoba. Lew returned to Ontario and on Feb 16, 1921, he married Margaret Taylor in Belmont. They returned to Manitoba where they lived with Philip and Sena and Lew's three daughters until they ultimately returned to Ontario. Lew operated a business: Abbott, Mity and Cann Co. Ltd, in Ingersoll in the 1930s. He is listed as a dairyman residing with his wife, Margaret, at 506 Central Avenue, in London, on the 1935 Voters List and later in 1945 as a grocer at 565 Central Avenue.

When their son and his family returned to Ontario, Philip and Sena remained in Treherne. In the 1926 Census of Manitoba, Saskatchewan and Alberta, Philip and Sena Abbott are described as "lodgers" living with the newly married Lulu and Melvin Harland in the Macdonald District, South Norfolk Municipality, Manitoba[94]. As they had done for periods of time in Ontario, they lived with each of their daughter's families, in turn, for several months and then moved on to another daughter's home. One might wonder if this arrangement

Philip Abbott (1858-1934)

was mutually satisfactory, but I have heard it described by several of their grandchildren, who have vivid recollections of their Grandpa and Grandma Abbott living with them. It was just the way things were.

A photo of Sena with her 3 youngest daughters was taken at the home of Grace Abbott Vennard in the 1930s. We can see Grace, Lulu and Alma with Sena (seated), with the Manitoba landscape in the background.

Grace Abbott Vennard, Lulu Abbott Harland, Alma Abbott Henry with Sena Abbott Baldwin (seated), c. 1934. From Margaret Abbott Shackleton's photo album.

Philip and Sena's second child Margaret (Maggie) May was born on May 23, 1888. Maggie married George Lorne Shackleton on January 1, 1906, at her residence at Glencolin, Malahide Township. Lorne and Maggie Shackleton lived for several years in South Dorchester on the Dunn Farm on the centre road to Aylmer. In 1918 they bought the William Abbott Farm from Fred Abbott, who had purchased some of the acreage and had some bequeathed to him by William Abbott in 1914. Lorne and Maggie Shackleton farmed and also operated a general store in Gladstone. Lorne served as Reeve of North Dorchester Township for several terms and was a member of the Thames River Conservation Authority.

Lorne and Maggie had ten children: Maurice Raymond (1907-1959), Stewart Lorne (1908-1963), Alma Laura (1910-1997), Hazel May (1911-2015), Dorothy Ilene (1914-2015), Clayton Robert (1915-1975), Donald Ross (1917-2004), Harry Orville (1919-1969), Irma Louise (1921-1977) and Arnold Verne (1923-1992).

Maurice Shackleton married Stella Grose. Maurice and Stella raised their family on the neighbouring farm next to Maggie and Lorne Shackleton. They had William (Bill), Betty, Gerald, Donna Jean (Jean), Clifford, Carol, Linda and Wanda. Bill married Norma Gilbert and their children were Bonnie, Penny, and Michael. Betty married Raymond Dance and they had David, Betty (Diane), Charles, and Marcia. Gerald married Anne Henderson and they later divorced. Their children were Gerald, Susan, Karen, Dennis, and Debra. Jean married William Putnam. They had Marylyne, Raymond, Cheryl, Robert, and Valerie. Clifford married Ethel Knott. Their children were Gord and Dan. Carol married Robert (Jim) Shiels. They had Randy, Brenda, and Barbara. Linda married Ron Brower. They later divorced. Their children were Donald and Mary Ann. Wanda married Andy Derewlany. They had Dana and Darrin. Maurice Shackleton died in 1959 and Stella died in 1988. They are *buried in Dorchester Union Cemetery.*

Stewart Shackleton married Grace Jackson. They lived in Belmont and ran the general store until they moved to Stratford where Stewart operated a farm equipment dealership. Their children were Frances (Elaine), Jackson (Wayne), Grace (Marie), Stewart James (Jim), Lois and Glen. Elaine married Ron Gibb. Their children were Nancy, Cynthia, Marjorie (Gail) and Charles (Andy). Wayne married Lorraine Dawson. They had Stewart, Kathryn, Glenna (Jane) and Brent. Marie married Bob McDonald. Their children were Robert (Dean), Joan, and Rodney. Jim married Constance (Connie) Pretty. They had Brian, Ian, Joan, and Judy. Lois married Doug Aitchison. They had two daughters, Heather and Jacqueline. Glen married Karen Coulthard. They had three sons, David, Scott and Derek. Stewart Shackleton died in 1963 and Grace Shackleton died in 2000. They are buried in Dorchester Union Cemetery.

Alma Shackleton married Murray Malpass. The Malpass family were neighbours, living on the 5th Concession, of North Dorchester Township. Alma and Murray lived in London on Belgrave Avenue. Murray worked for a bread company, first as a driver, and later, as an office manager. They had Nancy and William (Bill). Nancy married Morris Murchison of Windsor, Ontario. They had Joan and David. Morris was a Canon of St. Paul's Anglican Cathedral in London after serving as a Rector in many parishes in the Sarnia and Ottawa areas. Bill married Jean Culp. Their children were Lynn and Todd. Bill was awarded the Queen Elizabeth II Diamond Jubilee medal for service to his community. Alma Malpass died in 1997 and Murray died in 2004. They are buried in Dorchester Union Cemetery.

Hazel Shackleton met Gordon Ferguson of London, Ontario when she played softball for Labatt's, Kellogg's, Silverwood's and several other teams in the London Industrial Leagues in the 1920s. They were married on December 31, 1932 and moved to Toronto, where Gordon had been transferred by Dunlop Tires, in early 1933. They had Robert (Bob) Gordon, Douglas Colin and Gail Susan and raised their family in the Beaches neighbourhood. Bob Ferguson was born in Toronto in 1935. He graduated from the University of Toronto in Civil Engineering and worked his entire career with the City of Toronto and Metro Toronto, rising to the position of Commissioner. Bob married Rose Mary Wecsey in 1962. They had Geordon, Catherine and Kirsten. Geordon married Corinne (Corey) Ginou. Catherine's partner is Ralph Deketele, and Kirsten married Iain Andrews. Douglas Ferguson was born in Toronto in 1940. He worked as a music teacher for the East York Board of Education and inspired countless students to perform in the school marching band. At one time he took a busload of students to the Calgary Stampede. Douglas married Mary Elizabeth Starr in 1963. They had two sons, Dean Colin and Kent Douglas. Gail Ferguson was born in Toronto in 1953. She met Joseph George Romain at the University of Western Ontario School of Library and Information Science in 1980. They both graduated with a Master`s degree in Library Science. Gail worked as a librarian for the Toronto Public Library for 27 years. Joseph was Curator of *The Hockey Hall of Fame* and librarian for the Ontario Multifaith Council before returning to public librarianship just prior to retirement. He is the author of several novels and non-fiction books. Gail and Joseph lived together for twenty-three years and had three children: Breeze Susannah,

Lionel Joseph and Simone Rose, before marrying in 2004 in Toronto. Breeze married Ewan Rose. They had Callum Joseph. Lionel married Juliana Metolli. Their son is Archer Aleksander. Gordon Ferguson died in 1976 and Hazel died in 2015 at the age of 103. They are buried in Highland Memory Gardens, Toronto, Ontario.

Dorothy Shackleton married Elmer Garton. The Garton family were neighbours, living on the 6th Concession, North Dorchester Township. After their marriage, Dorothy and Elmer lived in Belmont and later in Ingersoll where Elmer worked for Borden's Milk Company. They were long time members of Trinity United Church in Ingersoll and Dorothy was a member of the Rebekah Lodge. She enjoyed playing cards and cheering on the Toronto Blue Jays. They had Margaret, Donald (Don), Gary, and Dorothy (Marlene). Margaret married Ray Pogue. Their children were Denise, Donna, and Darryl. Don married Rosalene Chambers. They later divorced. Their children were Karen, Scott, Larry, and Carolyn. Gary married Mary Schreurs. They had Amy, James, and Glen. Marlene married Brian Travis. They had two sons, Bradley and Sean. Elmer Garton died in 1980 and Dorothy died in 2015 at the age of 100. They are buried in Dorchester Union Cemetery.

Clayton Shackleton attended Ontario Agricultural College in Guelph, Ontario on a scholarship and later worked as a food inspector in Montreal where he met Wilma Willows, a registered nurse. Clayt and Wilma were married in Montreal in 1942. Their children were Robert, Mary Evelyn, Patricia (Pat) and Clayton Roy, who died in infancy. Robert married Sylvia Houghton. Their lifelong work has been in alternative healthcare services. They had one daughter, Destiny. Mary Evelyn married Terry Buist. They had two sons, Andrew and Christopher. Pat married Garry Willis. They later divorced. They had Carolyn, Robin, and Jaret. After a long partnership, Pat married Tom Wolsey in 2012. Pat had a very successful spa business for several years and Tom is a rancher. They have a large blended family. Clayton died in 1975 from the cumulative effects of Multiple Sclerosis. Before his death, he willed his body to the University of Toronto, Division of Anatomy. He is buried in St. James Cemetery and Crematorium, Toronto, Ontario.

Donald Shackleton married Louise Jackson. Louise was the daughter of Dennis and Edna (Cline) Jackson of North Dorchester Township. She grew up in a very musical family and played piano by ear. Don and Louise farmed on the 8th Concession in Malahide Township. They had Marilyn, Ron, Ruth, Edna (Lorraine), David, Mary (Diane) and Donald (Larry) and Joyce. Marilyn married Doug Walker. They had one son, Mark. Ron married Carol Williams. Their children were Deborah, Jeffrey, Terence, and Allan. Ruth married Harry

Hewbank. They had Karyn, Kimberly, Nancy, and Timothy. Lorraine married Ron Odanski. They had one son, Trevor. Lorraine and Ron later divorced. Lorraine married David Tuff. David Shackleton married Lisa Underhill. They had Lisa and Robert. Diane married Wayne Burgess. Their children were Leslee, Darryl and Charlene. Larry married Renee Rommel. They later divorced. Joyce married Ross Crawford. They had two children, Scott and Krista. Donald died in 2004 and Louise in 2014. They are buried in Springfield Kinsey Cemetery.

Harry Shackleton was a healthy, active child when he contracted Polio at the age of eight. In spite of so many medical difficulties throughout his life, he had many accomplishments. Harry attended Ontario Agricultural College in Guelph, Ontario, graduating in 1940. During World War II he worked at the Connaught Laboratories in Toronto, supervising the production of plasma. While working in Toronto, Harry boarded with his sister, Hazel, and her husband, Gordon, and travelled to work by public transit. It was during his daily commute that he met Florence McKee at a streetcar stop. They eventually married in 1948. From 1946 to 1954, Harry worked at the Provincial Health Laboratory in Windsor, Ontario. His work later took the family to Timmins, Ontario in 1955 when he worked at the Timmins Department of Health Laboratory for 5 years before returning to Toronto. Their children were Kevin and Margaret. Kevin is a birder, military historian and writer and intrepid explorer of his Shackleton ancestry. Kevin married Linda Sobon in 1982. They had Hilary, Joanna, and Christine. Hilary married Colin Cooke. They have one daughter, Adelaide. Harry died in 1969 in Windsor, Ontario. Florence later married Howard William Schedewitz in 1985 in Kitchener, Ontario. He died in 1991. Florence died in 1997 in Toronto. Harry and Florence are buried in Dorchester Union Cemetery.

Irma Shackleton was a very talented singer as well as a piano and organ player. She had a great sense of style and always appeared well dressed and coiffed. Irma worked for various branches of the federal government in London, Ontario. Irma married John (Jack) Love, the son of Peter and Eva Love of Delaware Township. Irma and Jack lived near Lambeth, Ontario. They had a daughter, Loralee, who seemed to inherit her mother's sense of style and her talent for music. Loralee married John Aarts. Together they operated an excavating business. They had Ryan, Jonathan, and Kevin from John's first marriage. Their sons continue to operate the company. Irma died in 1977. Jack died in 1993. They are buried in McArthur Cemetery in Elgin County.

Arnold Verne, known as Verne, was a dairy farmer. He also had a strong entrepreneurial spirit and bought and sold several properties including the old Gladstone schoolhouse. Verne married Blanche Hawley. They farmed just south of Gladstone, Ontario. They raised six children: Judy, Janet, Norman, Brenda, Bruce and Paul. Judy married Dennis Brown. Their children were Neil, Calvin, Sheila, and Randy. Judy later divorced from Dennis. Her partner is Gary Gill. Janet married Jim Rigsby. Their children are Hawley and Alex. Norman married Ethel Lamb. They had three children, Erin, Jane, and Thomas. Brenda married Dave Dale. They had three sons, Robert, Gregory and Steven. Bruce married Sharon Wintermute. They had Laura and Christopher. Paul has a daughter, Mauricia. Verne Shackleton died in 1992. Blanche died in 2007. They are buried in Dorchester Union Cemetery.

I have heard many stories about Maggie Abbott Shackleton from my mother Hazel and my Aunt Dorothy. Many of these stories apply to so many farm women in southwestern Ontario in the early 20th century. Maggie had a large garden from which she harvested fruits and vegetables that saw her large family through the winter. Both of her daughters Dorothy and Hazel recall how proud she was of her fruit cellar. They describe how she would take visitors down into the cellar to see her 100's of jars of preserves. Another craft was making wicker baskets. Willow was picked and then soaked to make it pliable, the frame was made of willow stakes and then longer pieces were woven to form the bowl of the basket and the handle. Some of the deeper baskets were used to corral baby chicks who were too weak to remain in the barn. They were brought inside the house and fed bread soaked in warm milk. Maggie would put them in a deep basket so they wouldn't run about. One time after rushing about feeding and caring for them she sat down in a chair and realized too late that she had crushed some of them who had climbed out of the baskets. She cried over that in frustration.

Maggie had a sewing machine in the kitchen and made clothes for the family often adding some decorative extra such as a bolero or vest to a dress. She loved to bead blouses and made the beautiful blouse that her sister Ruby wore on her wedding day. A highlight of the week was Sunday dinner when she would invite families from church to join her family around the large dining room table.

Maggie was a member of the Harrietsville Women's Institute. In 1929, in her role as President of the Women's Institute, she led a quilting project that represented all the families in the Harrietsville community. Maggie Abbott Shackleton taught her children to hook rugs and would admonish them to keep at it when they worked on large projects like the rug for the double parlour.

Margaret Abbott Shackleton and family circa 1935. Rear from left: Harry, Stewart, Alma, Clayton, Irma, Don, and Verne. Front from left: Hazel, Lorne, Maurice, Maggie, and Dorothy.

Lorne Shackleton bought a general store in Gladstone from R.A. Wilton in the 1920s. Many of the Shackleton children worked in the store, but eventually preferred to earn wages and found work elsewhere. Dorothy was in Grade Ten when she had to leave school to work in the store with her mother. There was much to learn. Everything had to be weighed and two phone lines managed as the store was mid-way between the Belmont and Harrietsville exchanges.

Shackleton's General Store in Gladstone, circa 1928. Photo courtesy of Margaret Abbott Shackleton's photo album. Irma (and possibly Clayton) Shackleton are pictured here in front of the store.

Maggie's friends were her neighbours and nearby relatives: the Kingwells, the Abbotts, the Presseys, Longfields and Tapsalls. Maggie's sisters, Ruby and Ellen, helped her with her large family. Visits with her sisters Alma, Grace and Lulu were few but she went to visit them in Manitoba on several occasions. Maggie died of heart disease on February 27, 1949, in St. Joseph's Hospital in London, Ontario. Lorne died in 1964 leaving an estate[95]

Philip Abbott (1858-1934)

that disinherited several of his children. Although the family was devastated, it eventually recovered from the damage. Maggie and Lorne are buried in Dorchester Union Cemetery.

Philip and Sena Abbott's third child was Ellen Alzina, born March 25, 1890. Ellen had a beautiful singing voice. She married William Ewart (Earl) Houghton on October 23, 1912, at the home of Maggie and Lorne Shackleton. The Houghtons lived in the Glencolin area of Malahide Twp. North Gore, Lot 32. They had six children in seven years. Ellen may have been overwhelmed and was treated for stress in a mental health hospital. The family can be seen in the 1921 Census of Canada with six children and Earl Houghton's brother Glenn. Lamentably, their children were sent to live with other families soon after, followed closely by the sudden death of Earl Houghton on December 9, 1922, due to a ruptured appendix. Earl was buried in South Park Cemetery just south of St. Thomas, Ontario.

Ellen eventually recovered from her illness, the adoption of her children, and the death of her husband. She worked as a household helper and lived with Maggie and Lorne Shackleton and their large family. She was a loving person who babysat Maurice and Stella Shackleton's children, among many others. She was in some ways more of a grandmother to them than their own grandmother. She was well loved by her nieces and nephews. Some would say that she was exploited, as she worked in exchange for her room and board. Ellen later lived with the Jim and Annie Kingwell and their family in Harrietsville. Eventually, she lived in a nursing home where she died on March 8, 1972. Ellen was buried in Springfield Cemetery.

Regrettably, Ellen and Earl's children were separated and raised in adoptive families. William Ewart Houghton was raised by his Uncle Ira and Aunt Twyla Houghton. He married Leah Ketchabaw and they had: Roy, Ronald, Donna, Carol, Glen, Lee, Jean, and James. Russell Carson Houghton was raised by the Walls family in Port Talbot, and later by the Knott family. He later worked for Laura Shackleton. Russell married Jean Dunbar and they raised Sylvia, Vernon, Mary, Richard, Thomas, and William. Harold (Houghton) Young was adopted by the Young family. Harold married Hazel Newman. Their children are Jack, Gloria, Douglas, Sharon, and Peter Young. Bruce Houghton and his sister Edna were adopted together by a kindly family of two unmarried sisters and a brother who lived south of Aylmer. Their name is not known. Bruce married Marion Sneddon. Their children are David and Rosemary. Edna married Ansel Martindale and had seven children: Thomas, Betty Jean, Shirley, Dorothy, Robert, Pat, and Daniel. Ethel Houghton was adopted by Rev. and Mrs Taylor.

Her name was changed to Marion. She married Frank Sypher and they also had seven children: Sylvia, Frank, Bob, Russell, Michael, Frederick, and Colleen.

Ruby Abigail Abbott was the fourth child of Philip and Sena Ann. She was born on October 26, 1896, Ruby was fifteen when her parents moved to Manitoba. She remained in Ontario to help her sister Maggie with her growing family. She met and eventually married John Shackleton (Shackelton), the brother of Maggie's husband, Lorne Shackleton, on December 15, 1920. Ruby raised Carmen Shackleton, John's son by his deceased first wife, Bertha McIntyre Shackleton, and three more children: Vera, Kenneth and Leslie. Ruby and John farmed on Concession 10, Lot 5, in South Dorchester Township. This lot was previously owned by Sarah Jane Brooks and George Woolley, John Shackleton's grandparents. Catfish Creek flowed through their property. They moved to a neighbouring farm when their son, Ken, took up farming. In retirement, John and Ruby moved to John Street in Aylmer. Ruby died on June 30, 1974, and John died on January 3, 1982. They are buried in Springfield Kinsey Cemetery.

Ruby and John's daughter, Vera, was born on Christmas Day, 1921. She married Ernest Parsons in 1943. They had 6 children: Walter and Wayne (twins), Leonard, Leon, and Myrna and Verna (twins). Walter married Connie Brown. They had Michael and Darby Parsons. Wayne married Marie Richardson. They had Christopher, Richard, Lena and Jesse. Leonard married Jackie Essay. They had Jeff and Melissa. Myrna Parsons married Robert Budden. They had Tracey and Byron. Myrna later divorced Robert and married Charles Hough. Verna Parsons married Barry Stratton. They had two sons, Danny and Trevor. Vera Parsons was an avid family historian and wrote history and community news articles for local newspapers. Kenneth Shackleton married Leone Silverthorn. They had Jessica, Laura, Sharon, Brian and Mark. Jessica married Wayne Wilson. They had Lisa, Karalee and Jeffrey. Jessica and Wayne later divorced. Laura married John Strickler. Sharon married William Ross Dean. They had Scott, Krista and Rebecca. Brian Shackleton married Mary Jane Martin. They had Julie. Mark Shackleton, and his wife Susan, had Darren. Leslie (Les) married Dorothy Hunter. Their children are John, Douglas, Gwendolyn and Gary. John Shackleton married Ronee Hammond. They had Michael, Jeffrey, Jason and Cameron. Doug Shackleton married Debbie Anderson. They had Jay and Wendy. Gwendolyn Shackleton married Robert Tracey. They had Tyler, Mark and Ashley. Gary Shackleton married Kim Hudson. They had Mallory-Lyne, Caylee, and Whitney.

Grace Agnes Mary Abbot, the fifth child of Philip and Sena Abbott, was born on June 9, 1898, in Elgin County, Ontario. She married John Vennard in South Norfolk, Manitoba near Treherne on October 24, 1917. John was the son of Matthew and Elizabeth Graham Vennard. Matthew Vennard was one of fifteen children. He was born in Elgin County, Ontario, just after his parents had emigrated from Belfast, Northern Ireland. Elizabeth Graham was born near Owen Sound, Ontario. Matthew homesteaded and built a home in the Arbroath District and then brought his wife west from Ontario. Matthew Vennard donated the land to establish the Rossendale Cemetery. Elizabeth Vennard was the local midwife. John and Grace Vennard took over the home farm from John's parents in 1917 and lived there for fifty-seven years, eventually building a modern home which replaced the original farmhouse. John Vennard met Grace Abbott while playing baseball. Both Grace and John were very involved in their community. John was a member of the Canadian and Manitoba Hereford Breeders Associations for over fifty years. He also served on the local school board, hospital board and municipal council. Grace participated in local sewing circles and helped to organize annual picnics for the local women's association.

John and Grace had four children: Elsie, Norman, Raymond and Donald. During the war years (1939-1945) their sons, Norman and Raymond, served overseas and Donald worked on the family farm. Elsie had graduated from the University of Manitoba in 1938 and worked at the local branch of the Bank of Montreal. Elsie married Leonard (Len) Wilke. When Len returned from overseas, they moved to a farm outside Regina. They had five children: Linda, John, Wendell, Reginald and Sheila. Norman Vennard married Beatrice English. They lived in the Arbroath District and raised a family of five children: Wendy, Patrick, William, David and Donna. Raymond Vennard married Erna Petersen. They had two children: Alexander and Doris. Donald Vennard purchased an adjoining property to his parent's farm and farmed the home farm as well. Living there with his mother after the death of John Vennard on November 5, 1974. John and Grace Vennard celebrated their 50th wedding anniversary on October 24, 1967. Grace Vennard died on September 29, 1983. She is buried with John in Rossendale Cemetery, Rossendale, Manitoba.[96]

Alma Abbott, the sixth child of Philip and Sena, was born on June 6, 1900, in Aylmer, Ont. She came to Manitoba with her mother and two sisters, Grace and Lulu when she was about fourteen years old. Alma became a young housekeeper in the home of Robert and Adeline Henry, original homesteaders in the Rossendale hamlet area. They had a large six bedroom brick home which still stands in 2018. In this family, she met and later married her husband, Clarence Henry on Oct. 6, 1917. Alma and Clarence had four children: Ruby, Vera, Douglas and Robert. Ruby married Bert Scammell. They had Jim, Sandra, Barry, John, Jean, Delmer and Robin. Vera Henry married Fred Bowles. Their children were Garry and Donald. Douglas married Connie Woodward. They had Terry, Joanne, Steven and Dennis. Robert married Marjorie Delf. They had Linda, Roberta, Bob and Barbara.

Clarence and Alma lived and farmed very near the South Rossendale School for a number of years, but moved to the Henry farm when Clarence's parents retired from farming. Clarence and Alma continued to farm there until Clarence was in his seventies and then later rented out the land. Their family held their sixtieth wedding anniversary in the Rossendale curling club in 1977. In their early 1980s, they moved into the village of Treherne and rented a small home for the winter months, returning to their farm in the spring. Later they bought a home in the village where they lived on a full-time basis.

Alma loved to sing, dance and listen to her music. She grew a large garden each year which included strawberries and raspberries. When her children had grown, she would have her Winnipeg grandchildren and great-grandchildren come to spend time in the summer months. She was a lifetime member of the Rossendale United Church Women's Auxiliary. She enjoyed reading the Reader's Digest and doing word puzzles. During a number of winters, Alma would come to live in Winnipeg. She worked for Eaton's mail order service and at times would do short term stints as a housekeeper and child care provider. On occasion, she enjoyed travelling to Ontario with her sisters, Grace and Lulu to visit her siblings and cousins.

Clarence Henry died in Treherne Hospital on July 4, 1982. Alma remained living in their Treherne home and was close to her sisters, Grace and Lulu until their deaths. In 1987, due to failing health, she moved into the Personal Care Wing of the Treherne Hospital. Alma passed away on May 31, 1989. Alma and Clarence Henry were buried in the Rossendale Cemetery with many of their family and extended family members.[97]

Philip Henry Warren Abbott, the seventh child of Philip and Sena Abbott, was born on March 23, 1902. He died only a few days later on March 27, 1902, in Malahide Township[98].

Lulu Loretta was Phillip and Sena's youngest child. She was born on October 29, 1903, at Aylmer, Ontario. At the age of eight, she came with her parents and two sisters, Grace and Alma, to the Treherne, Manitoba area. Lulu married Melvin Harland on December 17, 1924, and they rented a farm one and a half miles south of the Harland Farm. Melvin and Lulu farmed here until 1938, when they purchased a half section farm one mile west and a mile south, in the Matchetville District. In 1944 Lulu and Melvin moved to the Harland Farm north of Treherne in the Arbroath district, which Lulu aptly named "Shady Lane." They lived there until retiring to Treherne in 1967.

Lulu and Melvin had three children, Robert (Harvey), Joyce Lucille and Melvin (Wayne). Harvey married Velma Lee. They had five children: Brad, Brian, Campbell, Paul, and John. Joyce married Ronald William Derkson. They later divorced. They had Dale, Kimberley, Roxanne, Brent, and Shaunalee. Tragically, Kimberley died in infancy. Wayne married Sharon Gay Paulishyn. He and Sharon had Tamara and Nicholas. Wayne was also the father of Lorinda, Delmer and Juli. Wayne and Sharon hosted the Western Abbott Reunion for several years. Wayne died on January 31, 2017.

Lulu worked right alongside Melvin on the farm, milking cows, hauling water, feeding livestock and driving horses. She always planted a huge garden and reaped the benefits by canning and putting down preserves for the winter months. She raised chickens and turkeys and made a renowned canned chicken dish. She loved to cook and bake and each year she was proud to enter her baking in the Treherne fair and often took home a prize. When Lulu and Melvin got their family automobile, Lulu was every bit as active driving it to family and community functions as she had been driving the horse and buggy. She never tired of picking up friends or family members, always ready to help them out as most of the other women in the community did not drive.

Although Lulu immersed herself in the Manitoba prairie farm lifestyle, she always had a yearning for Ontario, calling it "God's Country," and took every opportunity, which were few and far between in those days, to go back for a visit whenever she could. She truly missed her siblings and other relatives in Ontario. She even went so far as to order, each summer, a bushel of peaches from Ontario for eating raw and canning because, as she put it, "British Columbia peaches were just not near as tasty as Ontario's".

Lulu had a wonderful gift for music. She played the piano by ear and could usually play a piece just by listening to the first few bars. She often played for the Arbroath School Christmas concerts. She played the organ for the church and her alto voice could be heard in the church choir. Lulu loved playing cards. She and Melvin enjoyed hosting card games for friends and family, playing euchre, canasta and whist well into the night. Lulu was a member the Arbroath District Hospital Guild and Arbroath Community Club and the Treherne United Church, as well as being a life member of the Matchetville United Church Women's Club and the Legion Auxiliary, District No. 21.

Ruby, Lew, Lulu, Maggie, Ellen, with Joyce Harland (in front) at Treherne Railway Station, 1940.
Courtesy of Maggie Abbott Shackleton's photo album.

This very active woman was diagnosed with liver cancer and passed away at Treherne Hospital on November 26, 1971, at the age of 69 years. She had planned her funeral, right down to the finest details: who she wanted for her pallbearers, the hymns she wanted to be sung, and what dress and jewelry she would wear. Melvin died several years later on Nov 2, 1976, in Treherne. They are both buried in Bethel Cemetery, Treherne, Manitoba. [99]

Chapter 8
Edwin Abbott (1860-1927)

Edwin Abbott was the fourth son of William & Lydia Abbott. Born in Ermington, Devon on March 17, 1860, he was eleven years old when the family came to Ontario.

Edwin married Harriet Eaton (1859–1931) the daughter of James Eaton (1844-) and Mary Ann Moore Eaton (1848-). The Eatons were neighbours of the Abbotts in Gladstone. Witnesses at the wedding on March 2, 1887, were Edwin's brother Jack Abbott and Annie Lapthorne. Jack and Annie married a few days later on Mar 9, 1887.

Edwin and Harriet farmed on the 5th Concession, North Dorchester Township, just west of Harrietsville. They had four daughters: Mary Ann (1888-), Elva Lydia (1889-), Emma Myrtle (1891-), and Alberta Christina (Allie) (1892-). The 1901 Census of Canada indicated that Edwin and Harriet had adopted eight-year-old Albert Hubbard, who was born in Ontario on January 21, 1893. Whether or not this was a legal adoption is not known. They also employed an eighteen-year-old farm worker named Neil Stevens.

Believed to be Edwin Abbott, c. 1875. Photo courtesy of Charles Baldwin.

Edwin Abbott and Harriet Eaton on their wedding day, 1887. Courtesy of North Dorchester Heritage Book Committee.

In 1907 at the age of eighteen, Edwin and Harriet's eldest daughter Mary Ann or Maud as she was known (1888-1983), married James Pettit (1883-1953). They lived at RR 1 Belmont. Their children Gordon Ross (1910- 1981), Melvin James (1913-1986), and Leta Mary (1920-2015) all went to the Belmont Public and Continuation School. Later, Leta attended Wells Academy in London for secretarial training and married Peter Lawson (1916-1989). They had Mary Jean, Donna, and Diane. Gordon attended Westervelde School before settling into farming. Gordon married Madeline Arrand in 1934. They had Ronald. Melvin married Clara Ferguson. Their children were Ralph and Murray.

There are many Johnsons in the lives of Edwin and Harriet's daughters. Their second eldest daughter, Elva Lydia (1889-1912), married Murray Johnson (1887-1974) on April 7, 1909, in Harrietsville, Ontario. Murray was the son of William and Emily Johnson of Avon, Ontario. Elva and Murray lived with several other members of the Johnson family in Avon according to the Census of 1911. Tragically, Elva died shortly after giving birth to their only child, daughter Elva Erie Johnson in 1912. After several years Murray Johnson married Vera Andrew in 1919. Elva Erie (1912-1991) married Fred Pilkington in 1933 in Avon. They had Carol, Jerry, William, and Donna.

Edwin and Harriet's third daughter, Emma Myrtle (1891-1982), and her husband, Ezra Johnson (1888-1974) married in 1910. Ezra was the son of John and Jane Johnson and also the uncle of Murray Johnson who had married Emma's sister, Elva. Their son John Edwin (Johnny) was born in 1917 and passed away in 1994. He married Grace Morris (1919-2012). They had two sons, Ralph and Robert.

The youngest of Edwin and Harriet's daughter, Alberta Christina (Allie) (1892-1981) married Emerson Johnson (1889-1953) in Harrietsville in 1913. Emerson was the son of James and Mary (Whitesides) Johnson of Malahide. Allie and Emerson's daughter, Edna Arletta, was born in 1927. Edna married Gerald Winnington-Ingram in 1947. They lived in Aylmer, Ontario and had two children, Judy and Janet.

Two Abbott brothers: Believed to be John Rowse (standing) and Edwin (seated), c. 1880. Photo courtesy of Charles Baldwin.

By 1921, when Edwin and Mary Ann retired, they moved to Aylmer and lived in the north end of town near the old tobacco factory. Edwin maintained a pair of jersey cows which they kept for milk and butter. He is remembered with a corncob pipe resting at the corner of his mouth. His granddaughter, Leta, recalled that at one time Edwin was injured falling out of an apple tree. Two doctors attended him, but it was his wife, Harriet, who cared for him and got him back on his feet. Although he had always been a resilient man, Edwin died due to pernicious anemia which created a progressive weakness for two years before his death on August 11, 1927. Harriet died on January 24, 1931. They are both buried in the Dorchester Union Cemetery.

Chapter 9
Priscilla Rowse Abbott (1861-1935)

Priscilla Rowse Abbott was born in Ermington, Devonshire, England on May 23 1861[100]. She was the only daughter in a family of eight boys. Priscilla's mother Lydia died a short six months after the family arrived in their new home in Belmont, Ontario. Priscilla was just eleven years old at the time. As the sole female in a large family she would have had a particularly difficult time adapting to life in Ontario, so far removed from relatives in Devon.

Priscilla had a collection of small portraits of relatives, photographed in Devon. These may have been given to her before she emigrated, or may have been sent to her in Belmont, Ontario after the death of her mother. These photographs were sent to the author by Charles Baldwin. They appear in the first pages of this book. Only one of these can be identified with any certainty. It is a photo of Nellie Kingwell, a cousin of Priscilla's. On the verso is written, "Nellie Kingwell, for Priscilla".

At the age of twenty-five Priscilla married Warren Baldwin (1865-1939) son of Samuel and Abigail Ketchabaw Baldwin. The marriage took place at the home of Rev. D.G. Sutherland at 464 Park Avenue, in London, Ontario on September 28 1886. Witnesses to the marriage were Charles Kingwell of Dorchester, a cousin of Priscilla, and Helena A. Sutherland, presumably the wife or daughter of the minister[101]. It's interesting that the wedding took place in London and not nearer to Priscilla's home in North Dorchester or in Eden, Ontario, where Warren lived. There may have been no minister available to perform the marriage locally. Priscilla's brother Philip Abbott and Warren's sister Sena Ann Baldwin had married in 1885 at the Methodist Parsonage in Tillsonburg, Ont. Priscilla and Warren had been their witnesses.

Priscilla Rowse Abbott Baldwin, c. 1875. Photocopy courtesy of a display by Shirley Moody Franklin at the 100th Abbott-Kingwell Reunion.

After their marriage, Priscilla and Warren lived on the Baldwin Family farm at Maple Grove on the 8th Concession in Bayham Township. Priscilla was hardworking and known to be a kind, caring and compassionate wife. The Baldwins had four children: one daughter, Agnes Mary (1888-1969), and three sons, Charles Samuel, who died in infancy, William Vernon (Verne) (1897-1974), and Clarence Warren (Clare) (1903-1956). The Baldwins attended Bayham United Church. They lived with Warren's widowed mother Abigail Ketchabaw Baldwin (1843-1913). Abigail was the daughter of Jacob Ketchabaw and Susan Ammerman. She married Samuel Baldwin, her first husband, at the age of sixteen and had six children: Elzina and Agnes, both of whom died in infancy, Sena Ann, Warren, Mary Margaret, and Marquis. The 1891 Census provides a kind of four generational snapshot of the Baldwins with Warren and Priscilla, their three-year-old daughter Agnes and Abigail's seventy-two-year-old uncle Thomas Ammerman (1818-1901). At that time, Abigail was widowed and was head of the household[102].

The Baldwin's second child, Charles Samuel Baldwin was born in November of 1890, but sadly he died a few weeks later in December. By 1901 Priscilla and Warren were farming Lot 12 and 13 Concession 8. They continued to provide a home for Warren's great uncle, Thomas Ammerman, who had reached the age of eighty-three[103].

By 1911 their eldest child Agnes had married and Priscilla and Warren were farming and raising their two sons, Verne and Clare at Maple Grove, but by 1921 the family made room for a thirteen-year-old "adopted" daughter, Myrtle Dennis, who immigrated to Canada in 1915 at the age of seven years old. Myrtle was born in England and so were her parents. In the 1921 Census, she was originally described as a housekeeper, but this notation was crossed out. Myrtle may have been one of the 100,000 juvenile migrants, or Home Children, who came to Canada between 1869 and 1930, although her name was not found among the searchable nominal indexes[104].

Priscilla Rowse Abbott (1861-1935)

Priscilla Abbott Baldwin and family, c. 1915. Rear from left: Verne, Agnes and Clarence. Seated from left: Warren and Priscilla. Photo courtesy of Charles Baldwin.

Priscilla and Warren's daughter Agnes Mary married Charles Madison Kennedy on March 20, 1907. They lived at Maple Grove, Eden, Ontario. Agnes and Charles had five children: Nellie Geraldine, Ruby Dell, Erie Beatrice, Harley Russell, and Charles Lee. Nellie died in infancy. Ruby Kennedy married Dwight Moody. They had Gordon, Blake, Gerald, and Shirley. Dwight Moody died at the age of thirty two from injuries suffered in an automobile accident in October, 1938. Erie Kennedy married Reginald Stewart. They had Beverly, David, Daniel, Calvin, and James. Harley Kennedy married Hazel Jean Rennie. They had a large family of eleven children: Charles Arnold, Marilyn Agnes, Joyce Arlene, Lois Jean, Sandra Ann, Mary Alene, Gary Harley, Dianne Louise, Wayne Robert, Clinton Kenneth, and Brian Allan. Charles Lee Kennedy married Edna Gates and they had Walter Lee. In 1968 Charles Kennedy died and Agnes died a little more than a year later in 1969. Their daughter, Ruby (Kennedy) Moody did extensive genealogical research on the Abbott and Baldwin families which served as a legacy to future generations[105].

Priscilla and Warren's son, Verne, enlisted with the Canadian Army and joined the Western Ontario Regiment in May of 1918. Verne was twenty-one years old. He was ordered transferred overseas to England in July of 1918, but the order was cancelled the following day[106]. Verne was later discharged in February of 1919 when the regiment was demobilized. Verne married Rebecca Faye Wilson in 1922. They had seven children: Nina Faye, William Llewellyn (Bill), Victor Donald, Ivan Lee, Charles Stanley, June Eunice and Wayne Maurice. Nina Baldwin married Arnold Ferris and they had Karen Ann. Bill Baldwin married Donna Marie Franklin. Their children were Donald William, Cheryl Louise and Warren Brent. Victor Baldwin married Lucille Small. They had Beverley Lucille, Dale Victor, Calvin and Melvin. Ivan Baldwin married Florence Corbett and they had a son named Corbett. Charles Baldwin married Marlene Longworth. They had three children: John Charles, Sarah Jane, and Stephanie Ann. Eunice Baldwin married Roger Tuck. They had Susan and Blair. Wayne Baldwin married Shirley Cornell. Their son is Jeffrey Wayne. Verne and Faye Baldwin were married for over fifty years. Verne died at the age of seventy-seven in 1974. Faye died in 1978. They are buried in Eden Cemetery.

Clarence (Clare) Warren Baldwin was born on February 12, 1903. He married Iva Merle Williams at the age of nineteen on his birthday, February 12, 1923, at the Baptist Parsonage in Eden, Ontario. On April 1, 1925, with only twenty-five dollars in their pockets, Clare and Iva and their daughter Lila moved to Detroit, indicating at the border crossing that they intended to live permanently in the U.S[107]. A cousin of Iva`s, Lee Williams, was their contact in Michigan. For reasons unknown and not stated in the official records, the couple and their young daughter didn't stay long in Detroit as their son Robert was born back in London, Ontario a little more than a year later in June of 1926. Clare and Iva had three children: Lila, Robert and Ronald. Lila Bernice Baldwin was born in 1924. Her first husband was Stanley (Bus) Jackson. There were no children from this marriage, but Lila later married Max Balkwell and had four children, Bonita (Bonnie), Robert, Brian and Wendy. Lila died in 1990. Clare and Iva's second child, Robert, was born in London, Ont. on June 21, 1926, and was tragically killed at the age of eighteen in an automobile accident involving a motorcycle and car collision on Highway 19, on June 23, 1944[108]. A second son, Ronald, was born in London, Ontario in 1932. Ronald married Anna Bandura. They had three sons: Timothy Lyndon, Daniel Morgan, and Ronald Samuel. Ronald applied and was approved to become a naturalized American citizen in 1967 in Tuscon, Arizona. Ronald died in 1999. Clare Baldwin died in 1956 and Iva died in 1960. They are buried in Eden Cemetery.

Priscilla Abbott Baldwin died following abdominal surgery on April 18, 1935, at the age of seventy-four. Warren continued to live on the farm at Maple Grove with his son Verne and his family. He died in 1939. In his later years, Grandfather Warren often wandered from the farm and his grandchildren were instructed to go and find their Grandfather and bring him home. This is one of the stories of Dr Charles Baldwin who wrote a memoir of growing up in the large Baldwin family during the Depression, entitled *Maple Grove and beyond… to Eden*. This book illustrates the vital sense of community that got people through the hardships of the 1930s[109]. Priscilla Abbott and Warren Baldwin are buried in the Eden Cemetery.

Chapter 10

John (Jack) Rowse Abbott (1863-1944)

John (Jack) Rowse Abbott was named for his paternal grandmother Priscilla Rowse. He was born on March 11, 1863, in Ermington Devon and came to Canada when he was eight years old. A young child of the immigrant family, he would have struggled to deal with the death of his mother, Lydia, and the many changes that the family experienced in their first few years in Ontario.

Jack married at the age of twenty four. His wife, Annie Lapthorne, was the daughter of John and Mary Lapthorne. Annie Elizabeth Lapthorne was born in London, Ontario on June 15, 1861. Her parents farmed in London Township before taking up the butchering trade in London, Ontario. Jack and Annie were married on March 9, 1887. The wedding took place at the Lapthorne home on the 3rd Concession of London Township. Jack's brother, Thomas Abbott, and Annie's brother, Frederick Lapthorne, were witnesses.

Annie's father, John Lapthorne, had emigrated from Devon, England and arrived in Canada in 1857. In Yealmpton Parish, Devon he had been a neighbour of the Abbotts and Lethbridges. When John Lapthorne was enumerated in British Census of 1851 at the age of twenty-two, he was working in Yealmpton as a servant at Orchard Farm owned by Grace Horton[110]. The Abbott and Horton families were related by marriage[111]. Having neighbours from Yealmpton, Devon, who were already settled and prospering in the London area, may have been one of the reasons why the Abbotts chose Belmont as for their future home. When the Abbotts emigrated in 1871 they were accompanied by Elizabeth Lapthorne. Elizabeth may have been the sister of John

Lapthorne who had emigrated from Devon in 1857. Elizabeth was not found in any of the common Canadian genealogical records in the years that followed, so, she may have returned to England.

John (Jack) Rowse Abbott and Annie Lapthorne, 1887. Photo courtesy of Loreen VanKoughnett and Margaret Dunn.

Jack and Annie had four children: Emerson Lapthorne (1888-1937), Frederick John (Fred) (1890-1952), William (Sherman) (1892-1944) and Elise Mary (1894-1980). They farmed Lot 18 on the 4th Concession in North Dorchester Township. Later, they also ran the Cheese Factory in Gladstone with their son Sherman.

In the Census of 1901, Emerson Abbott resided with his grandparents John and Mary Lapthorne. By 1911 the Census shows Annie's mother, Mary Lapthorne, living with Jack and Annie and their family. Mrs Lapthorne died in 1915. The 1921 Census shows Edwin Rowse, Jack`s second cousin, living on the next farm, Concession 4, Lot 17 with his family[112]. This neighbourly proximity demonstrates that the immigrant families remained close long after they settled in the area. (Edwin Rowse`s father John Lethbridge Rowse was Lydia Lethbridge`s first cousin).

Jack and Annie Abbott and family. Seated from left: Jack, Elise, Annie. Standing from left: Sherman, Emerson, Fred. Taken on Emerson Abbott's wedding day, 1916. Photo courtesy of Loreen VanKoughnett and Margaret Dunn.

Jack and Annie's eldest son, Emerson Abbott, married Teresa Demaray on May 17 1916. They had one daughter, Eula. Emerson was a trained cheesemaker and ran the cheese factory in Dorchester. Tragically, he drowned at Port Stanley on August 12, 1937, when his fifteen-year-old daughter, Eula, became caught in an undertow. Emerson jumped in the water to rescue her and suffered a heart attack. Eula survived, but Emerson drowned. The coroner, George H. Jackson, pronounced the cause of death to be "accidental drowning"[113].

Teresa Demaray Abbott kept the cheese factory business going for time, but eventually, it became more than she could manage. Her daughter, Eula, married Lewis Hunt and they farmed between Ingersoll and Thamesford. They had three children: George, Judith and Jim. Judith died in infancy, but the two boys were raised on the farm. When the farm was sold Eula and Lewis moved into Thamesford. George later moved to North Bay and Jim moved to Clinton Twp., Michigan.

Jack and Annie's second son, Frederick (Fred) was born on May 15, 1890. Fred married Elda Demaray in May of 1918. Fred and Elda lived on the family farm outside of Gladstone. Their daughter, Freda, and her husband Harvey Willsey lived in London. Their son, Donald Demaray Abbott, married Yvonne White. Donald took over the farm when Fred died and farmed for many years before moving to St. Thomas in 2006.

Jack and Annie's youngest son, William (Sherman) and his wife Anne Pyatt ran the Gladstone store when they were first married in 1919 and lived and worked there throughout the 1920s. Their daughter Loreen was born in Gladstone. The store burned down later in the 1920s and they switched to farming in Mosseley where their children Margaret and Ray were born. After two barn fires, Sherman and Annie moved back to Gladstone and ran one of two cheese factories in town. The Pressys ran the other cheese factory in the southern part of Gladstone. Three or four years later after the cheese factory failed they moved to a one hundred acre farm at Gladstone. The farm had two houses on it, which allowed Jack & Annie to live next door to their son and his young family. Loreen married Roy VanKoughnett in 1941. He went overseas in July of 1941 with the Royal Canadian Mechanical Engineers and was stationed in England. For the duration of the war, Loreen moved to her parent's home in Gladstone. When Roy returned in 1946 they moved into Ingersoll. Loreen was a seamstress and did custom sewing from her home and later at Crosby's Dress Shop in Ingersoll. Loreen and Roy had two sons: LeRoy and David. Roy died in 1998 and Loreen moved to London in 2003 to share an apartment with her sister Margaret. Loreen died in 2015. Sherman and Annie's daughter, Margaret, met Carl

Dunn in Gladstone where he taught school. They married in London and stayed there briefly before moving to Melbourne, Ontario. Later they moved to Sarnia where their son, Larry, was born. In 1959 the family moved to Toronto where Carl taught at the Teacher's College. The family returned to London and when Carl retired, they settled in Ingersoll next door to Loreen and Roy. Larry Dunn married Georgette De Caire. They lived in London and had two children Geoffrey and Cheryl. Carl died in 1988. Sherman and Annie's son, Ray Abbott, married Margaret Zavitz. He took over the family farm when Sherman died and lived there for many years raising his large family of six children: Archie Wayne, Marion Viola, William, Marilyn, Teresa and Carl.

Jack and Annie's daughter, Elise, married Howard Armstrong (1887-1971), and in 1922 they managed the Gladstone store. They had three sons, Jack Rowse, Gordon Wray and Murray. In 1925, little Murray, died. Elise and Howard moved to Detroit where their fourth son, William, was born. They often visited family in Ontario and for many years the extended family would celebrate Christmas together by renting a hall in Beechville. Howard died in 1971 and Elise died in 1980. They are buried in Dorchester Union Cemetery.

Referred to by everyone as Jack, John Rowse Abbott is remembered by his grandchildren as a big easy-going man who suffered badly from arthritis. He also had very poor eyesight, in fact, he was very nearly blind, but continued to drive well past the age he should have stopped. His grandchildren remember being volunteered to drive with Grandpa so they could tell him when to turn and when he was about to veer off the road. There were more than a few mishaps when Grandpa drove into ditches or hit a lamppost. With such profoundly impaired vision, he made good use of his other senses to manage his surroundings. He also refused most medications that were ordered by the doctor. Jack and Annie created a comic sight when they drove together as Jack was six feet tall and sat high behind the steering wheel, while Annie was quite a short woman and her diminutive stature made her seem to disappear below the dashboard. Her granddaughters said she was small but mightily strong-willed, and she frequently spoke her mind.

Jack Abbott died on April 6, 1944, at the age of eighty-one. Within six weeks of his death, his son Sherman died of cancer. On October 16, 1945, at the age of eighty-four, Annie Abbott arrived at the United States Border Crossing at Detroit, Michigan and applied to be granted permission to reside permanently in the United States with her daughter Elise Armstrong. The documents indicate that she had some degree of senility and that her vision was severely impaired.[114] Upon her death in 1959, Annie was buried with Jack in Dorchester Union Cemetery.

John (Jack) Rowse Abbott (1863-1944)

Chapter 11

Thomas Lethbridge Abbott (1867-1925)

Thomas Lethbridge Abbott was the only one of William and Lydia's children to be named for Lydia's family. He bore the name of his Grandfather, Thomas Lethbridge, (1796-1861). Thomas was born on January 20, 1867, in Ermington Devon. He was four years old when his family emigrated. He would have had barely a memory of his relatives in Devon and would have relied upon his sister and brothers after the death of his mother Lydia. He had a younger brother Charles and would soon have a new mother, Mary, and a new younger brother, Alfred, by the time he was of school age.

Thomas married Sarah Deacon (1866-1948) the daughter of William and Catherine Deacon who were hotel keepers in Clandeboye, Ont. in Donnelly country just north of the town of Lucan. Sarah's mother died of typhoid fever in 1873 when Sarah was seven years old and her father died five years later in 1878 when she was only twelve years old. Both of her parents were buried in the Southgate/O'Neill Cemetery near London, Ont. In 1881, at the age of sixteen, Sarah lived with William and Mary Ann O'Neill in London Township.

A record of the marriage of Thomas and Sarah has not been found, but it is known that they married on April 30, 1890, in Belmont[115]. Thomas worked in Belmont as a blacksmith at the forge of George Shultz. The Abbotts resided just outside of the village in Westminster Township Concession 7, Lot 1 in 1890[116]. Their son William Earl was born on March 8, 1895.

According to the 1901 Census the family had moved to Thamesford where Thomas worked as a blacksmith. William Earl was six years old but not yet attending school according to the Census data. By 1911, Thomas, Sarah and William Earl lived in Dorchester. William Earl, at age sixteen, was a blacksmith's apprentice to his father. According to the Census of 1911, Thomas held a life insurance policy that cost him $20.00 per year. Sometime between 1911 and 1918 the family moved to 303 Hale St. in London. As a young man, William Earl worked as a steam-fitter at the London Asylum.

Sarah Deacon Abbott, William Earl and Thomas Lethbridge Abbott, c. 1918. Photo courtesy of Bernard Kingwell.

On March 27, 1918, William Earl signed up for duty with the Western Ontario Regiment. He served as a Sapper with the Canadian Engineers in France. A Sapper is a skilled soldier who performs a variety of military engineering duties such as demolitions, bridge-building, and laying or clearing minefields, as well as working on road and airfield construction and various heavy repairs.

Military attestation papers of William Earl Abbott, signed at London, Ontario, March 28, 1918. Military file: Abbott, William Earl, Reg. number 3131217 © Government of Canada. Reproduced with the permission of Library and Archives Canada (2019). Source: Library and Archives Canada/RG150, Vol. 10-12, item number 270

In May of 1918, William Earl was transferred from London, Ont. to Brockville for basic training. He was sent to England in July and arrived in France in September. He was assigned to the 5th Battalion on September 28, 1918. Within five months of leaving home, he was killed in action on October 4, 1918. A *Circumstances of Casualty Report* indicates that he was "killed instantly while sleeping in his billet, a fragment of shell piercing his brain"[117]. William Earl Abbott was buried in Haynecourt Military Cemetery, (Plot 2, Row C, Grave 9) near Arras, France. A memorial service was held for William Earl in London, Ontario at St. Mark's Church on Sunday, November 10, 1918, ironically one day before the Armistice was signed on November 11th. Sarah Abbott was awarded a small amount of back pay, $60.00, as William had bequeathed his personal estate to her [118].

Sapper William Earl Abbott, Western Ontario Regiment, 1918. Photo courtesy of Charles Baldwin

Understandably, Thomas Abbott never seemed to recover from the loss of his only son. Thomas and Sarah moved to 581 Pall Mall, London, Ontario and Thomas worked as a blacksmith at the London Asylum for a few years. He died at the age of 58 in 1925 after suffering abscesses of the head followed by mastoid surgery in March of 1924. Sarah lived for many years following the death of her husband and died on April 21, 1948. They are buried together in Dorchester Union Cemetery.

At sunset November 4th through to sunrise November 11th, 2008 a vigil was held to commemorate the Canadians who lost their lives in World War I. The names of the 68,000 war dead were projected over a week of nights onto the National War Memorial in Ottawa, the Toronto City Hall, and several other buildings in other regions of Canada and onto the side of Canada House in Trafalgar Square in London, England. William Earl Abbott's name was projected simultaneously in Toronto and Ottawa. On November 7, 2008, at 5:31 p.m. William Earl's first cousin, twice removed, Kevin Shackleton, saw William Earl Abbott's name appear in Ottawa on the Canadian War Memorial and simultaneously, William Earl's first cousin, twice removed, Gail Ferguson, saw his name projected on the Toronto City Hall.

Chapter 12

Charles (Charlie) Henry Abbott (1869-1950)

Charles Henry Abbott, c. 1900. Photo courtesy of Loreen Vankoughnett

Charles (Charlie) Henry Abbott was the youngest child born to William Abbott and Lydia Lethbridge. He was born in Yealmbridge, Devon on June 17, 1869. Charlie would have had no memory of life in England since he was only two years old when the family emigrated.

Charlie waited quite a while to marry. He married Sara McCord who was born in Stewartstown, Northern Ireland, on February 28, 1871. They married on June 27, 1900, in Belmont, Ontario. Charlie was thirty one and Sarah was twenty-eight. Their marriage registration tells us that Sara's parents were Joseph McCord and Elizabeth Greer, from County Tyrone, Northern Ireland[119]. Sara appears on a Ships Passenger List from 1875. The family arrived in Quebec on board *The Sardinian*. Sarah was one of eight McCord children.

According to the Census of 1921, Charlie and Sara farmed on Concession 5, Lot 22 of North Dorchester Township[120]. They had three children: William Joseph, born on Sept 18, 1907, Mary Elizabeth Greer born on Nov. 14, 1910, and Charles Keith born on

Aug. 10, 1912. In the 1911 Census, William Joseph was three and Mary Elizabeth Greer was not yet a year old. They employed a fifteen-year-old girl named Mary Pilbey as a domestic servant or helper.

Sara McCord and Charles Henry Abbott on their wedding day, June 27, 1900. Photo courtesy of Loreen VanKoughnett and Margaret Dunn.

Charles and Sara Abbott and Keith, Mary and William, c. 1915. Photo courtesy of Mary Abbott Collection.

Charles (Charlie) Henry Abbott (1869-1950)

The Abbotts farmed and raised their children along the road between Gladstone and Belmont. Charlie has been described as "a real Abbott": always interested in what was going on and wanting to be a part of it. The Voters List for 1935 describes Charlie as an "agent". Later, in a 1940 Voters list Charlie, Sara, Mary and Keith are living at R.R. 1 London, Ontario. Keith is listed as a trucker and Mary as a teacher. Charlie died on July 7, 1950, in London and Sara died on June 24, 1953, in London, They are buried in Dorchester Union Cemetery.

Their eldest son, William Joseph, married Gladys Rose Holdon on May 27, 1950, in London at the age of forty-three. A Voters List for 1968 shows William J. Abbott, clerk, and his wife, Gladys, librarian, living on Base Line Rd. in London. Another list of electors has William J. Abbott living in East London, on Lawson Road married to Gladys R. Abbott, retired in 1974. William died in 1976 at the age of 69. There is a William J. Abbott buried in Oakland Cemetery in Mosa, Township.

Charles and Sara's daughter, Mary Elizabeth Greer, was a school teacher, an artist and a family historian. She developed a generational family chart entitled *The Abbott Family by Mary E. Abbott, June 1965*. Mary died in 2003.

By 1957, Charles and Sara's youngest son, Keith and wife Elsie [sic Margaret Elise] Hodgins lived at 358 Boler Ave. in Byron and Keith's sister, Mary, lived nearby at 364 Colville Blvd. In 1968 Keith and Elsie owned a hardware store. Elsie died in 1986 followed by Keith in 1992. They are buried in Dorchester Union Cemetery.

Chapter 13
Alfred (Fred) Abbott (1873-1943)

Alfred (Fred) Abbott was the only child of William Abbott and his second wife, Mary Victoria Evans. He was born on Oct 28, 1873, into a family of eight siblings.

Fred was thirty-three years old when he married Elizabeth Rickard, (1884-1964) on June 6 1906. Witnesses at the wedding were Beatrice Sales, cousin of the bride, Maurice Abbott, a nephew of the groom, and the flower girl was Gladys Gee, a niece of the bride. Elizabeth Rickard came from a family of nine children. Her father, Philip Hendy Rickard had been born in North Dorchester Township to English parents. Elizabeth's mother, Elizabeth Sadler Rickard was also Ontario born. Her family had farmed in Middlesex County since at least the 1850s. The Rickards farmed in North Dorchester with their large family and later moved to the village of Dorchester.

Fred and Elizabeth Abbott farmed with William and Mary Abbott in North Dorchester on Concession 6, Lot 18. They had three children: Harold Alfred, John Maxwell (Max) and Mary (Jean) Elizabeth. In 1918 Fred and Elizabeth sold their farm to Lorne Shackleton. In 1921 the Abbotts lived at 971 Colborne Street, in London, Ontario. Fred's occupation at that time was a carpenter. In 1928 the Abbotts bought a one hundred acre farm at Concession 5, Lot 7 West Nissouri Township. In 1930 their eldest son, Harold, purchased this farm and Fred and Elizabeth moved to a house at 5 St. George Street, in London.

Fred Abbott, Beatrice Sales, Elizabeth Rickard, Maurice Abbott and Gladys Gee. Photo courtesy of Marlyn Brady.

140 *The Abbotts*

Max, Jean and Harold Abbott, c. 1912. Photo courtesy of Marlyn Brady.

Alfred (Fred) Abbott (1873-1943)

Fred and Elizabeth's eldest son, Harold Alfred Abbott, was born on July 13 1907. On July 2, 1932, Harold married Norine Innes of Glencoe, Ontario. Norine was born on Aug 12, 1912. They farmed in West Nissouri Township on the farm that Harold purchased from his parents. Until 1956 the farm consisted of a herd of Jersey cattle and a number of hens and swine. In 1956 the jerseys were replaced by Purebred Holsteins. In 1967 Harold Abbott & Sons purchased a neighbouring farm. Harold and Norine had four children: Joyce, Marlyn, Gerald, and Ronald. Joyce Elizabeth Abbott was born in 1933. She married Kenneth John Fortey on May 4, 1957. Ken worked for Sumerville's Supertest and later for Canada Trust. Joyce was a mother and housekeeper. Joyce and Ken's family are Kenneth (Wayne), Brian John, Karen Norine, June Elizabeth, and Kelly Ann. Harold and Norine's second daughter is Marlyn Norine, born in 1937. Marlyn married Raymond (Ray) James Cross on May 18, 1957. Marlyn and Ray's children are Brenda Norine and Bradley Raymond. Ray was a police officer in Sarnia for twelve years. Marlyn raised her family and later worked on the farm. In 1968 they returned to West Nissouri Township to join the Abbotholme Farm Partnership until 1984 when they semi-retired to Monteith Avenue in Thorndale. In early 2002 Ray was diagnosed with bone cancer and he passed away on April 21, 2002. In April of 2005, Marlyn met William (Bill) Milburn Brady. They were married in May of 2006. Bill's lifetime career was with Bell Canada. He retired in 1989 and later developed a candle lamp business.

Harold and Norine's eldest son, Gerald (Jerry) Maxwell Abbott was born in 1939. Jerry married Jacquelin Elizabeth Drager on Aug. 20, 1966. They divorced in 1968. Jerry then married Ruth Helena Richardson. At the time of their marriage, they built a new house on Glanworth Road. Jerry owned Abbott Trucking until he retired in 2007 and Ruth taught at the Arthur Voden High School in St. Thomas until her retirement in 1997. They hosted the Abbott-Kingwell Family reunion at their home for many years.

The youngest of Harold and Norine's children was Ronald (Ron) Harold, born in 1940. Ron married Mary Margaret (Marg) Lockwood on July 27, 1968. Ron returned to the family farm after graduating from Ridgetown Agricultural College. He farmed with his parents under Harold Abbott & Sons and later under Abbotholme Farms until 1984. In 1990 Ron and Marg sold the farms and purchased 50 acres on the west side of Cobble Hills Road where they built a new house. Ron did a lot of ironwork as well as growing nursery stock. Marg did office work for many years. She died in 2017. Harold Abbott died on Dec 23, 1969, and Norine Abbott died on Oct 15, 1997. They are both buried in Dorchester Union Cemetery.

Fred and Elizabeth's younger son was John Maxwell (Max) Abbott, born on July 29, 1909. Max was teaching in Toronto when he married Kathleen (Kay) Elnora Gee on July 4, 1934. Max and Kay had one child, Kathleen (Kathy) Ann Abbott. Kay died on May 9, 1972. Max later married Margaret Ellen Ferguson on Oct 21, 1976. Max taught English and Geography at Central Technical School in Toronto. In the late 1970s, Max and Margaret moved to Richmond Hill. Margaret died in September of 2002 and is buried in Toronto. Max died on July 5, 2006. Kathy Ann Abbott followed her father into teaching. She taught primary grades and later taught children with behavioural problems and learning disabilities. When she retired, she continued to tutor.

Fred and Elizabeth's daughter was Jean Abbott, born on March 15, 1912. Jean married Elmer William Duffin on Oct. 4, 1941. They had one child Robert (Bob) William born in 1945. Elmer lived on the Duffin farm at Concession 3, West Half Lot 7 West Nissouri Township and farmed with his brothers. Jean was a school teacher and later a music teacher in public schools throughout West Nissouri Township. Bob Duffin married Bernice Kathern Clark. They had three children: Mark Robert, Kimberley Ann and Joseph (Joe) William. After graduating from Ridgetown Agricultural College, Bob returned to farming. He and Bernice worked on their farm in West Nissouri Township until they semi-retired in 2007 and sold their farm, moving to the Duffin Homestead where they built a new home on the site of the old house. [121]

Alfred (Fred) Abbott, William Abbott's youngest son, died on Jan. 23, 1943 of pneumonia. Elizabeth Rickard Abbott died on Aug. 28, 1964. They are both are buried in Dorchester Union Cemetery.

Chapter 14
The Abbott Legacy

William Abbott emigrated from Devon England in 1871 at the age of thirty-nine. He was the only one of his six siblings to leave Devon. From what I have learned of him, I believe that William was quite a risk taker. He made the decision to emigrate in order to own land and make a better life for his family and their descendants. He had little expectation that he would be able to achieve these goals in Devon.

This photograph of William Abbott, by Westlake of London, Ontario was taken some time between 1887 and 1901. Judging by his facial features, hair colour, and hands, he would have been about seventy at the time the portrait was made. William appears to hold a rolled document in his left hand, perhaps meant to represent a deed to the land ownership that he had pursued from Devon to Ontario. His posture is relaxed and his face reveals that he is content with his life and accomplishments. Although he doesn't appear to have been a man of large stature, he was strong, having pursued physically demanding occupations working as a blacksmith and later as a farmer. William Abbott died on October 16, 1914, as a result of a concussion. It has been said that he fell from a roof at the age of eighty-two, further evidence that he was a vigorous and very determined man throughout his life.

William Abbott c. 1900. Photo courtesy of the North Dorchester Heritage Committee.

William married Lydia Lethbridge and later, Mary Victoria Evans, and had nine children. He pursued his craft and supported his family as a master blacksmith, in Devon and later, in Ontario. Three of his sons apprenticed and later entered the trade during their working years. After only six years in Canada, he purchased a one hundred acre farm on Concession 6, Lot 18, North Dorchester Township near Gladstone Ontario and he became a successful farmer. By 1894, after bringing his family of eight children to Canada as immigrants, six of them were represented in the Directory of North Dorchester Township as freeholders or tenants. Within twenty-five years of arriving in Canada, William had built a spacious new farmhouse situated on well-cultivated and productive acreage. William Abbott really personified the Canadian immigrant dream.

At the time of his death in 1914, William Abbott's estate was valued at roughly $23,000. That amount would be worth $515,583.00 in 2019 Canadian Dollars. His real estate holdings were valued at just under $5000. His properties included about one and one half acres of Part of Concession 6, Lot 18, North Dorchester (the farm that he purchased in 1877); Lots 3 to 10 in Block 22, of Mount Royal in the town site of Swift Current, Saskatchewan; Lots 21 and 22 in Block 8 in the Parish of St. Boniface, Winnipeg, Manitoba; and Part Lot 8 and all of Lot 9 on the north side of Catherine Street in Dorchester, Ontario.

William's son, Fred, was one of the executors of William's Last Will and Testament and looked after the sale of the real estate in Dorchester. William's wife Mary was left $1000.00. Additionally, in a codicil, Fred Abbott was left one-half acre of the north-west corner of the 6th Concession, Lot 18, in North Dorchester Township where he resided with his own family and where his mother, Mary Victoria Abbott, resided until her death in 1918[122]

According to the letters of probate, William Abbott held two mortgages at the time of his death, one to Alfred Abbott for $6000.00. This was the balance owing from the purchase of Concession 6, Lot 18. The second mortgage for $3,500.00 to John Abbott for the purchase of Concession 4, Lot 19, North Dorchester. These debts were both repaid by the time the final accounting was submitted.

By 1918, portions of his estate had not been sold, namely the lots in Swift Current and St. Boniface. In addition, there were ten preferred shares in Siemon Co. Ltd., Toronto, which were valued at $1000.00. These shares could not be sold, presumably, because their value had dropped. The company, which had built furniture and flooring in Wiarton and Toronto, had experienced several bankruptcies during the war years and although the case was presented to the Supreme Court of Ontario in November of 1916, and was decided in favour of William Abbott's estate, the money was never realized. There were several other assets of outstanding promissory notes and securities.

William left his estate equally divided among his children and the family of his son, William, who had predeceased him. He left $2000.00 to each of them. Philip, Edwin, John and Alfred had previously received their shares. As stipulated in the will, the balance of his assets were divided among his seven sons. His daughter, Priscilla, received her $2000.00 legacy, but did not share in the division of the balance.

William Abbott's broader legacy was raising, with his two wives, Lydia and Mary, a family that continued to make contributions to Canada's economy and to Canadian society. The Abbotts moved beyond Elgin and Middlesex Counties in Ontario and Southwestern Manitoba, pursuing careers in agriculture and commerce, science and the arts, health and caring professions, and in the trades. They are teachers and truckers, civil servants and soldiers. They are what Canada is made of and just like their immigrant great grandfather, they don't flinch when opportunity knocks.

The Abbotts supported each other through the Great Depression and through two World Wars as the original Abbott descendants born in Canada made way for further generations. The family grew and they remained close. As this story goes, they began to gather for an annual family reunion in 1910 and continued to reconvene each year, and ultimately, celebrate their centennial in 2010. That is a long run for a celebration of family. Many of them remain connected as neighbours or over longer distances with phone calls and more recently with electronic media. They share stories, catch up on news, and feel connected as members of a large family. Since this story began with the narrative of the Abbott-Kingwell Reunion, it seems fitting to leave it here. The Abbotts were an immigrant family that made contributions to their new country in many more ways than I have recounted and while this narrative ends, their story continues.

Endnotes

1. C1871 England Census, Yealmpton, District 15, page 34.
2. The Historical Gazetteer of England's Placenames. http://placenames.org.uk/id/placename/08/008990
3. 1861 England Census, Ermington, District 18, page 4.
4. "England Marriages, 1538–1973 ," database, *FamilySearch* (https://familysearch.org/ark:/61903/1:1:N25Z-Q9V : 10 February 2018), Richard Abbott and Mary Philips, 15 May 1751; citing Dean Prior, Devon, England, reference , index based upon data collected by the Genealogical Society of Utah, Salt Lake City; FHL microfilm 917,195.
5. "England Births and Christenings, 1538-1975," database, *FamilySearch* (https://familysearch.org/ark:/61903/1:1:JMPZ-B2K : 11 February 2018, Richard Abbott, 02 Mar 1699); citing , index based upon data collected by the Genealogical Society of Utah, Salt Lake City; FHL microfilm 916,764.
6. "England Marriages, 1538–1973 ," database, *FamilySearch* (https://familysearch.org/ark:/61903/1:1:N25Z-Q9N : 10 February 2018), Richard Abbot and Jane Pearse, 12 Jan 1724; citing Dean Prior, Devon, England, reference , index based upon data collected by the Genealogical Society of Utah, Salt Lake City; FHL microfilm 917,195.
7. Baptism: "England Births and Christenings, 1538-1975," database, FamilySearch (https://familysearch.org/ark:/61903/1:1:JMPZ-B2K : 11 February 2018, Richard Abbott, 02 Mar 1699); citing , index based upon data collected by the Genealogical Society of Utah, Salt Lake City; FHL microfilm 916,764.
8. "England Marriages, 1538–1973 ," database, *FamilySearch* (https://familysearch.org/ark:/61903/1:1:NKY7-ZJS : 10 February 2018), Gulielmus Abbot and Gratia Veal, 13 Jun 1693; citing Buckfastleigh, Devon, England, reference , index based upon data collected by the Genealogical Society of Utah, Salt Lake City; FHL microfilm 916,764.
9. "England Births and Christenings, 1538-1975," database, FamilySearch (https://familysearch.org/ark:/61903/1:1:J36M-K6R : 11 February 2018, William Abbut in entry for Joane Abbut, 29 Dec 1695); citing , index based upon data collected by the Genealogical Society of Utah, Salt Lake City; FHL microfilm 916,764.
10. "England Births and Christenings, 1538-1975," database, *FamilySearch* (https://familysearch.org/ark:/61903/1:1:J36V-RMP : 11 February 2018, Mary Abbot, 05 Mar 1697); citing , index based upon data collected by the Genealogical Society of Utah, Salt Lake City; FHL microfilm 917,195.

11 © Copyright 2018 Newfoundland and Labrador Heritage Web Site, The West Country, http://www.heritage.nf.ca/articles/society/west-country.php.

12 The West Country by Gordon Hancock, c. 2000. Heritage Newfoundland and Labrador. https://www.heritage.nf.ca/articles/society/west-country.php

13 "England Births and Christenings, 1538-1975," database, *FamilySearch, FHL microfilm 917,195*

14 http://justus.anglican.org/resources/bcp/1662/Kindred1949.htm

15 Irish/Butler Family Tree, Huntington Family Tree, Wheadon Family Tree, 1 ENH DNA 17, Gutteridge-Turner Family Tree, Hyne family tree posted on Ancestry.com

16 England & Wales, Non-Conformist and Non-Parochial Registers, 1567-1970. RG4: Registers of Births, Marriages and Deaths, Devon, Wesleyan, Piece 0840: Ashburton Circuit (Wesleyan), 1820-1836

17 1841 England Census, District, Plympton St Mary, Sub-registration district: Yealmpton

18 1851 England Census, Devon, Plympton St Mary, 4b

19 Tithe Apportionment for the Parish of Plympton St. Mary, in the County of Devon, 1840. Tithe Apportionments from IR 29/6, 9, 10, 30 (The National Archives) © Crown copyright images reproduced by courtesy of The National Archives, London, England.

20 Kingwell, Bernard. *The Abbott Family Tree: Devon England to first generation born in Canada,* Willowdale, Ont.: Bernard Kingwell, 1985.

21 England & Wales, National Probate Calendar (Index of Wills and Administrations), 1858-1966, Priscilla Rowse Abbott, 1892.

22 1891 England Census, Devon, Plympton St. Mary, District 2.

23 England and Wales National Probate Calendar for 1858-1966, 1973-1995. Probate letters of Alfred James Abbott, died January 10, 1950.

24 https://www.gravestonephotos.com/public/namedetails.php?grave=293081&forenames=Frederick&surname=Lethbridge

25 General Register Office: Birth Certificates from the Presbyterian, Independent and Baptist Registry and from the Wesleyan Methodist Metropolitan Registry; Class Number: RG 5; Piece Number: 200

26 Devon County Council, Tithe Apportionment, Ermington Parish, Woodland Farm, https://new.devon.gov.uk/historicenvironment/tithe-map/ermington/

27 1841 England Census, Devon, Ermington, Dist. 15, pg.2.

28 1851 England Census, Devon, Ermington, Dist. 8A, pg. 36

29 Peter B. James. A brief chronological history of St. Austin's Priory Cadleigh, (near Ivybridge, Devon) 1912-2012.

30 Sharon and Stephen Murphy, owners of Cadleigh Manor, Ivybridge, Devon.

31 The Times, London: June 12, 1891.

32 England & Wales, National Probate Calendar (Index of Wills and Administrations), 1858-1966, 1973-1995, Thomas Lethbridge, 1861.

33   England, Devon. Marriages in the registration district of Plympton St. Mary, 1854

34   Imperial Gazetteer of England and Wales, edited by John M. Wilson. Edinburgh: A. Fullarton, 1870.

35   Output, Employment, and Productivity in the United States after 1800. Dorothy S. Brady, ed., NBER, 1966. ISBN: 0-870-14186-4 http://www.nber.org/books/

36   Floud and McCloskey (ed.) Economic history of Britain since 1700. Cambridge, England: Cambridge University Press, 1994.

37   Wylie, William. The Blacksmith in Upper Canada, 1784-1850: a study of technology, culture and power. Gananocque, Ont.: Langdale Press, 1990.(pp.51, 58)

38   *The Canadian News* of March 25, 1875 In a report of the Minister of Agriculture, which was laid before the Senate the other day, we find the following paragraphs:—" The combination of steamship companies, commonly known as the North Atlantic Conference, broke up on the 7th May last, from differences among its own members. The combination had for some years previously maintained the steerage or immigrant fare on steamships at the uniform rate of £6 6s. steerage to all parts in Canada and the Northern United States. Thus any steamship lines, parties to the conference, would take an emigrant to Boston or New York for £6 s6., and pay the intervening railway fare to Quebec; or, if the emigrant were landed at a Canadian port he would be taken to Boston or New York for the same fare. After the rupture of the conference, the steerage fare practically fell to what could be obtained, but the prevailing rate was £3. This state of things continued throughout the year. The arrangement that had been made by the department with the Allan, and the Dominion, the Temperleys, and the Anchor Lines, to afford passenger warrants to approved immigrants to Canada at the rate of £4 15s., remained in abeyance, in consequence of the rupture of the conference. A special warrant, however, enabing [sic] families of agricultural labourers and female domestic servants to obtain passages for £2 5s., became in very great demand."

39   CPI Inflation Calculator http://www.in2013dollars.com/us/inflation/1871?amount=30

40   Ancestry.com. *Canadian Passenger Lists, 1865-1935* [database on-line]. Provo, UT, USA: Ancestry.com Operations Inc, 2010.

41   Ontario. MS 6913, Assisted Immigration Register, 1870-1877. RG 11-3, volume 2 [Hawke Papers].

42   http://www.archives.gov.on.ca/en/microfilm/hawke_background.aspx

43   [*A short history of Belmont*, a paper given in 1932 by Mrs. E.E. George, Convenor of Historical Research Department of the Women's Institute.], from the Tweedsmuir History of Elgin County, http://www.elgin.ca/ElginCounty/CulturalServices/Archives/tweedsmuir/Belmont/page%200021-0024.pdf

44   https://www.archeion.ca/village-of-belmont-fonds

45   Letter from Mae Leonard Report to Charles Baldwin, May 28, 2010, Otterville, Ontario.

46   Ontario. Registration of Deaths, 1869-1938, MS 935, Reel 3, #029868

47   Ontario. Marriage Registrations, 1873, #008200.

48   1850; CENSUS PLACE: PYMATUNING, MERCER, PENNSYLVANIA; ROLL: M432_796; PAGE: 122B; IMAGE: 121

49   1901 Census of Canada, Middlesex, Dist. 87, Dorchester, A-6.

50   1861 Census of Canada West, Elgin County, Yarmouth, C-1019, Page 127.

51   Ontario. Middlesex County. Land Registry. Instruments and Deeds, 1877. No. 6660, Pg. 889.

52 Canadian CPI Inflation Calculator https://inflationcalculator.ca/

53 Canadian County Atlas Digital Project, North Dorchester, Illustrated historical atlas of the county of Middlesex, Ont. Toronto: H.R. Page & Co., 1878.

54 Census of Canada, 1881, Middlesex East, Dist. 167, Sub. Dist. Dorchester North B2, Page 17, Household 91. Library and Archives Canada, # 4278238. https://www.bac-lac.gc.ca/eng/census/1881/Pages/item.aspx?itemid=4278238

55 Census of Canada, 1891, Ontario, Middlesex East, Dist. 90, Sub. District, A, Division 2, Page8, Household 38. Library and Archives Canada.

56 Ontario. North Dorchester Abstract Index, Index to Deeds, Vol. A, 1866-1954, GS 350 mfm.

57 Census of Canada, 1911, Ontario, Middlesex East, Dist. 95, Sub. Dist.2, Page 7, Household number 81. Library and Archives Canada, item # 6225734. https://www.bac-lac.gc.ca/eng/census/1911/Pages/item.aspx?itemid=6225734

58 Ontario; Registrations of Deaths: MS935; Reel: 199, #020467.

59 London Free Press. Oct 17, 1914.

60 Ontario. Middlesex County [Land Record] Copybooks, Dorchester Pt. Lot 8 and all of Lot 9, (Plan 274).

61 Ontario. Middlesex County Estate file #11935, 1914-15, MS887, Reel 1341. Estate of William Abbott.

62 Immigration Information from the Province of Ontario, Department of Agriculture and Public Works, Archibald McKellar, Commissioner,1872.

63 Selected passages from Marjorie P. Kohli, Waterloo, Ontario, Canada, 1997-2010. http://jubilation.uwaterloo.ca/~marj/genealogy/thevoyage.html

64 1871 Census of Canada, Dorchester North, Middlesex East, Ontario; Roll: C-9904; Page: 54; Family No: 180

65 1871 Census of Canada, Dorchester North, Middlesex East, Ontario; Roll: C-9904; Page: 47; Family No: 155

66 1851 Census of England and Wales, Devon, Yealmpton, 7b, page 17.

67 Canadian County Atlas Digital Project, Middlesex County (Ontario Map Ref #5), Illustrated historical atlas of the county of Middlesex, Ont. Toronto: H.R. Page & Co., 1878.

68 1861 Census of Canada West, Middlesex, Enumeration District 1, St. Lawrence Ward, Township of London, Page 3.

69 England and Wales, Civil Registration Marriage Index, 1837-1915, Q3, 1945, Vol.9, Page 434.

70 1901 Census of Canada, Ontario, East Middlesex, Dist. 87, Sub Dist.,F-1, West Nissouri

71 London East, http://lstar-education.com/pages/london_east-history.htm

72 Ontario Surrogate Court, Middlesex Estate of William Abbott, application for Probate, MS 887, Reel 1341, no. 11935, Nov. 17, 1914

73 1921 Census of Canada, Ontario, London, District 101, Sub-district : 47 - Ward 4; *Polling Division no. 62*

74 Ontario, Death Registrations, 1927, Reg. #021951.

75 Ruby Moody's Family tree and Mary Abbott's Abbott Family list.

76 England & Wales, Non-Conformist and Non-Parochial Registers, 1567-1970, RG8: Registers of Births, Marriages and Deaths Plymouth, Piece 0008: Plymouth Circuit, Ebenezer Chapel (Wesleyan Methodist): Baptisms, 1837-1863.

77 1861 Census of England and Wales, RG 9 Folio 65 Piece 1429, Page 4 Family 23

78 Ontario. County of Middlesex, Division [Township] of Westminister, 1877, Schedule B Marriages, Archives of Ontario; Series: *MS 932_24*; Reel: *24*.

79 Illustrated Historical Atlas of the county of Middlesex, Westminster. Toronto: H.R. Page and Co., 1878.

80 1881 Census Canada, Ontario, District 167, East Riding Middlesex, Sub District 2 North Dorchester Twp., page 13.

81 North Dorchester Township Papers, Lot 24, Concession 6, Belmont, Nugent's Survey, subdivision lots 3 and 10. Page 288.

82 London City and Middlesex County Directory, 1890. London: R.L. Polk, 1890.

83 London City and Middlesex County Directory, 1887. London: R.L. Polk, 1887.

84 London City and Middlesex County Directory,. London: R.L. Polk. 1892 and 1894.

85 1891 Census Canada, Ontario, District #92, South Middlesex, Sub-Dist. #1, Westminster.

86 1911 Census Canada, Ontario, Waterloo South, Sub-District 14 – Galt.

87 1921 Census of Canada, Ontario, Reference Number: *RG 31*; Folder Number: *71*; Census Place: *Ward 2, London, Ontario*.

88 Canada. Federal Voters' List, 1965.Hamilton, Wentworth.

89 U.S., World War I Draft Registration Cards, 1917-1918, Michigan; Roll: 1675135; Draft Board: 01

90 Canadian Expeditionary Force (CEF), Regimental number 2356128. RG 150, Volume 04 – 16, Item Number: 107

91 1940 United States Census, Blackman Township, Jackson, Michigan, United States; citing enumeration district (ED) 38-3, sheet 6B.

92 Joy Salmon Moon interview, Muskoka, Ontario, c. 2007.

93 Michigan, Death Certificates, 1921-1952," index, *FamilySearch* (https://familysearch.org/pal:/MM9.1.1/KF3Z-CJD .

94 Census of the Prairie Provinces, 1926 for Image No.: e011221547, RG31, Statistics Canada

95 Ontario. Elgin County Estate file #18363, 1964, Estate of George Lorne Shackleton.

96 With thanks to Grace Abbott Vennard who contributed the history of the Vennard family to The Treherne Area History Committee's 1976 publication, *Tiger Hills to the Assiniboine*.

97 With thanks to Don Bowles, who provided Alma Henry's biographical information.

98 Mrs. Abbott's Book. Sena Ann Baldwin Abbott, c. 1930, (photocopy).

99 With thanks to Joyce Harland, who provided Lulu Harland's biographical information.

100 England & Wales, Civil Registration Birth Index, 1837-1915, 1861 Q2-Apr-May-Jun.

101 Ontario, Marriage Registrations, 1801-1928, 1933-1934, Middlesex 1886.

102 1891 Census of Canada, Dist. 60, Elgin East, Sub. Dist. Bayham

103 1901 Census of Canada, Elgin East, District 57, SubDistrict, Bayham, B-6.

104 1911 Census of Canada, Ontario Elgin East Sub-District 4 – Bayham.

105 Ruby Moody interview, Bayham Township, Elgin County, Ontario, c. 1998

106 Library and Archives Canada; Ottawa, Ontario, Canada; *CEF Personnel Files*; Reference: *RG 150*; Volume: *Box 386 - 54*, 1914-1918, BAJ-BAN, Box 0386. [Baldwin, William Verne].

107 Detroit Border Crossings and Passenger and Crew Lists, 1905-1963, M1478 - Detroit, 1906-1954, 1925.

108 Ontario. Death Registrations, 1944, #038327.

109 Baldwin, C. S. Maple Grove and beyond … to Eden: memoirs of the "comin'-up years" of C.S. (Chuck) Baldwin. Ridgetown, Ont.: Dr. Charles Baldwin, 2000.

110 1851 Census of England and Wales, Devon, Yealmpton, 7b, page 17.

111 William Abbott's (1832-1914) brother Philip Abbott (1834-) married Harriet Hamlyn Horton (1836-1863)

112 1921 Census of Canada, Ontario, Middlesex East , Sub-District 05 - Dorchester North

113 Ontario, Canada, Deaths and Deaths Overseas, 1869-1946 for Emerson Abbott, **Elgin , 1937**

114 UniteD States, Border Crossings and Passenger and Crew Lists, 1905-1963, M1478 - Detroit, 1906-1954

115 Kingwell…, Abbott Family Tree.

116 1891 Census of Canada, Ontario , Dist. 90 Middlesex East , Division 3A Dorchester North, page 1.

117 Canada, War Graves Registers (Circumstances of Casualty, 1914-1948 for William Earl Abbott). RG 150, 1992-93/314,Vol. 145.

118 Canada. Library and Archives. Canadian Expeditionary Force, Soldiers of the First World War, 1914-1918. Attestation papers. RG 120, Vol. 10-12, Item #270.

119 Ontario, Marriage Registrations, 1801-1928, 1933-1934, 1900.

120 1921 Census of Canada, Ontario , Middlesex East, Sub-District 05 - Dorchester North

121 *With thanks to Marlyn Abbott Cross Brady* for biographical information about Alfred Abbott.

122 Ontario Surrogate Court, Middlesex, application for probate file MS 887, Reel 1341, #11935, registered Nov. 12, 1914, probated Nov. 14, 1918.

Bibliography

Abbott, Mary E. Mary Abbott's Abbott Family list. (photocopy).

Abbott, Sena Ann Baldwin. Mrs. Abbott's Book. c. 1930, (photocopy).

Baldwin, C. S. Maple Grove and beyond … to Eden: memoirs of the "comin'-up years" of C.S. (Chuck) Baldwin. Ridgetown, Ont.: Dr. Charles Baldwin, 2000.

Bowles, Donald. Alma Henry's biographical information.

Brady, Dorothy S. (ed.).Output, Employment, and Productivity in the United States after 1800. NBER, 1966. ISBN: 0-870-14186-4 http://www.nber.org/books/

Brady, Marlyn Abbott Cross. Alfred Abbott's biographical information.

Canadian County Atlas Digital Project, North Dorchester, Illustrated historical atlas of the county of Middlesex, Ont. Toronto: H.R. Page & Co., 1878. Rare Books and Special Collections, McGill University Library.

The Canadian News, March 25, 1875.

City of London and County of Middlesex Gazetteer and Directory, 1874-75. London: Irwin and Co., 1874.

Floud and McCloskey (ed.). Economic history of Britain since 1700. Cambridge, England: Cambridge University Press, 1994.

Harland, Joyce. Lulu Harland's biographical information.

Hunt, Eula. Eula Hunt interview, Ingersoll, Ontario, 2018.

Illustrated Historical Atlas of the county of Middlesex, Westminster. Toronto: H.R. Page and Co., 1878.

Imperial Gazetteer of England and Wales, edited by John M. Wilson. Edinburgh: A. Fullarton, 1870.

Irish/Butler Family Tree, Huntington Family Tree, Wheadon Family Tree, 1 ENH DNA 17, Gutteridge-Turner Family Tree, Hyne family tree posted on Ancestry.com

James, Peter B. A brief chronological history of St. Austin's Priory Cadleigh, (near Ivybridge, Devon) 1912-2012.

http://justus.anglican.org/resources/bcp/1662/Kindred1949.htm

Kingwell, Bernard. The Abbott Family Tree: Devon England to first generation born in Canada. Willowdale, Ontario: Bernard Kingwell, 1985.

Kohli, Marjorie P. Selected passages. Waterloo, Ontario, Canada, 1997-2010. Immigration Information from the Province of Ontario, Department of Agriculture and Public Works, Archibald McKellar, Commissioner,1872. http://jubilation.uwaterloo.ca/~marj/genealogy/thevoyage.html

London City and Middlesex County Directory. London: R.L. Polk, 1887, 1890, 1892, 1894.

London East, http://lstar-education.com/pages/london_east-history.htm

Lovell's Business and Professional Directory of the Province of Ontario for 1882. Montreal: John Lovell and Son, 1882. Library and Archives Canada, OCLC 317478134

Mae Leonard Report to Charles Baldwin, May 28, 2010, Otterville, Ontario.

Moody, Ruby. Ruby Moody's Family tree. (photocopy).

Moody, Ruby. Ruby Moody interview, Bayham Township, Elgin County, Ontario, c. 1998.

Moon, Joy S. Joy Salmon Moon interview, Muskoka, Ontario, c. 2007.

Newfoundland and Labrador Heritage Web Site, The West Country by Gordon Hancock, c. 2000. Heritage Newfoundland and Labrador. https://www.heritage.nf.ca/articles/society/west-country.php

Province of Ontario Gazetteer and Directory, Including the City of Montreal, P.Q. 1895. -- Toronto: Might Directory Co., 1895.

[A short history of Belmont, a paper given in 1932 by Mrs. E.E. George, Convenor of Historical Research Department of the Women's Institute.], from the Tweedsmuir History of Elgin County, http://www.elgin.ca/ElginCounty/CulturalServices/Archives/tweedsmuir/Belmont/page%200021-0024.pdf

Treherne Area History Committee. Tiger Hills to the Assiniboine. Treherne, Manitoba: 1976.

Vankoughnett, Loreen and Margaret Dunn. Loreen Vankoughnett and Margaret Dunn interview, Ingersoll, Ontario, c. 2007.

Wylie, William. The Blacksmith in Upper Canada, 1784-1850: a study of technology, culture and power. Gananocque, Ontario: Langdale Press, 1990.

Index

100th Abbott-Kingwell Reunion see Abbott-Kingwell Reunion, 2010
Aarts, John : 104
Aarts, Jonathan : 104
Aarts, Kevin : 104
Aarts, Loralee Love see Loralee Love
Aarts, Ryan : 104
Abbotholme Farms : 142
Abbott Family : 107
Abbott Family Tree: Devon England to First Generation born in Canada : xii
Abbott Legacy : 144
Abbott Row : 32
Abbott Trucking : 142
Abbott tombstone, St. Peter and St. Paul Church, Ermington, Devon : 53
Abbott, Ada Clare (Ada Reading) : 92, 93, 94
Abbott, Albert : 3, 13, 71, 77, 86, 87, 88, 130
Abbott, Alberta Christina (Allie Johnson) : 114, 116
Abbott, Alfred : 38
Abbott, Alfred (Fred) : 69, 75, 76, 77, 80, 101, 139, 140, 143, 146
Abbott, Alfred James (1865-1950) : 40
Abbott, Alma Coral (Alma Henry) : xii, 98, 100, 110, 111
Abbott, Anne Pyatt see Anne Pyatt
Abbott, Annie Lapthorne Abbott see Annie Lapthorne
Abbott, Beatrice : 38
Abbott, Beatrice (Beatrice Cox) : 99
Abbott, Beverly John : 89

Abbott, Blanche : 38
Abbott, Bonnie : 7
Abbott, Charles (Keith) : 3, 135, 137, 138
Abbott, Charles Henry (Charlie) : 3, 13, 71, 135, 136, 137
Abbott, Chester Cleveland : 92, 94, 95
Abbott, Clara : 38
Abbott, Donald Demaray : 7, 128
Abbott, Donald Thomas : 89
Abbott, Edwin : 3, 13, 96, 114, 115, 117, 118
Abbott, Edwin Lewis (Lew) : 98, 99, 113
Abbott, Elda Demaray see Elda Demaray
Abbott, Eleanor : 27
Abbott, Eleanor (1847-1930) : 38, 40
Abbott, Elise Hodgins see Elise Hodgins
Abbott, Elise Mary Lapthorne (Elise Armstrong) : 7, 127, 129
Abbott, Elizabeth Rickard see Elizabeth Rickard
Abbott, Ellen Alzina (Ellen Houghton) : 3, 98, 99, 107, 108, 113
Abbott, Elsie Fox see Elsie Fox
Abbott, Elva (Elva Clark) : 99
Abbott, Elva Lydia (Elva Johnson) : 114, 116
Abbott, Emerson Lapthorne : 127, 128
Abbott, Emma Myrtle (Emma Johnson) : 114, 116
Abbott, Emmaline (1803-) : 20
Abbott, Emmaline (Emmaline Traher) : 26, 38
Abbott, Eula (Eula Hunt) : xiv, 7, 128
Abbott, Evelyn Bald see Evelyn Bald
Abbott, Evelyn Lydia (Eva) : 87, 88
Abbott, Freda (Freda Willsey) : 128

Abbott, Frederick (Fred) John Lapthorne : 127, 128
Abbott, Georgie Bratt : 92, 93, 94
Abbott, Gerald : 8, 142
Abbott, Gladys Emma (Gladys Wilson) : 87, 89
Abbott, Gladys Holdon see Gladys Holdon
Abbott, Grace (1729-) : 17
Abbott, Grace Agnes Mary (Grace Vennard) : xii, 98, 100, 110
Abbott, Harold Alfred : 139, 142, 143
Abbott, Harriet Eaton see Harriet Eaton
Abbott, Jacqueline Drager see Jacqueline Drager
Abbott, Joane (1695-) : 17
Abbott, John (1737-) : 17
Abbott, John (1805-) : 20
Abbott, John (Jack) Rowse : 2, 3, 4, 13, 25, 84, 96, 114, 117, 125, 126, 127, 129, 146
Abbott, John Maxwell (Max) : 143
Abbott, John Rowse (1840-1845) : 27, 38
Abbott, Joyce (Joyce Fortey) : 142
Abbott, Kathleen Ann (Kathy) : 143
Abbott, Kathleen Gee see Kathleen Gee
Abbott, Lillian Blanche (Lillian Priddle) : 92, 94
Abbott, Loreen (Loreen Vankoughnett) : xiv, 2, 4, 12, 128
Abbott, Lucille (Lucille Alexander) : 99
Abbott, Lulu Loretta (Lulu Harland) : xii, 98, 99, 100, 111, 112, 113
Abbott, Lydia Lethbridge see Lydia Lethbridge
Abbott, Lydie (Baby) : 64
Abbott, Margaret (Margaret Dunn) : xiv, 2, 4, 12, 128
Abbott, Margaret Ferguson see Margaret Ferguson
Abbott, Margaret Lockwood see Margaret Lockwood
Abbott, Margaret May (Maggie Shackleton) : 3, 98, 99, 101, 105, 106, 107, 113
Abbott, Margaret Taylor see Margaret Taylor
Abbott, Margaret Zavitz see Margaret Zavitz
Abbott, Marlyn (Marlyn Brady) Cross : xiv, 7, 12, 142
Abbott, Mary (1697-) : 17
Abbott, Mary (1742-) : 17
Abbott, Mary Ann (Mary Ann Kingwell) : 6, 27, 38
Abbott, Mary Ann (Maud Pettit) : 114, 116
Abbott, Mary Elizabeth : xii, 71, 77, 135, 137, 138

Abbott, Mary Jane Bratt see Mary Jane Bratt
Abbott, Mary Jean Elizabeth (Jean Duffin) : 139, 143
Abbott, Mary Page Parker see Mary Parker
Abbott, Mary Pearl (Mary Talbot) : 87, 89
Abbott, Mary Victoria Evans see Mary Victoria Evans
Abbott, Maurice : 38
Abbott, Maurice John : 87, 88, 89, 139, 140
Abbott, Maurice Leslie : 89
Abbott, Miriam (Miriam Yeoman) : 27, 38, 54
Abbott, Mity and Cann Co. Ltd : 99
Abbott, Norine Innes see Norine Innes
Abbott, Philip (1731-) : 17
Abbott, Philip (1801-1874) : 17, 18, 20, 25, 28, 29, 39, 40
Abbott, Philip (1834-1920) : 27, 38, 39, 40, 125
Abbott, Philip (1858-1934) : 7, 13, 96, 97, 98, 99, 119
Abbott, Philip (1901-1903) : 40
Abbott, Philip Henry Warren : 98, 111
Abbott, Priscilla (Priscilla Sandover) : 38, 40
Abbott, Priscilla Rowse (Priscilla Baldwin) : 3, 13, 80, 119, 120, 122, 124
Abbott, Ray : 128, 129
Abbott, Richard (1699-) : 17
Abbott, Richard (1724-1775) : 17
Abbott, Roger (1728-) : 17
Abbott, Roger (1764-1827) : 17, 18, 20
Abbott, Ronald : 6, 12, 142
Abbott, Ruby Abigail (Ruby Shackleton) : 3, 98, 99, 107, 109, 113
Abbott, Ruth Richardson see Ruth Richardson
Abbott, Sara McCord see Sara McCord
Abbott, Sarah Deacon see Sarah Deacon
Abbott, Sena Ann Baldwin see Sena Ann Baldwin
Abbott, Stuart Stirling : 92
Abbott, Sylvia Beatrice Anger see Sylvia Anger
Abbott, Teresa Demaray see Teresa Demaray
Abbott, Thomas Lethbridge : 3, 13, 85, 130, 131, 134
Abbott, William (1734-) : 17
Abbott, William (1799-) : 20
Abbott, William (1832-1914) : vii, xi, 6, 11, 13, 15, 18, 20, 25, 26, 39, 53, 54, 55, 58, 60, 64, 66, 71, 72, 77, 80, 91, 101, 144, 145
Abbott, William (Sherman) Lapthorne : 127, 128, 129

Abbott, William (no dates) : 17
Abbott, William -- Estate see Estate of William Abbott (1832-1914)
Abbott, William Earl : 130, 131, 132, 133, 134
Abbott, William Joseph : 135, 137, 138
Abbott, William Jr. (1856-1887) : xiv, 13, 14, 71, 72, 80, 90, 91, 92
Abbott, Yvonne White see Yvonne White
Abbott-Kingwell Reunion : xi, xiv, 1, 2, 4, 6, 85, 147
Abbott-Kingwell Reunion, 1922 : 3
Abbott-Kingwell Reunion, 1940 : 4
Abbott-Kingwell Reunion, 1948 : 5
Abbott-Kingwell Reunion, 1958 : 6
Abbott-Kingwell Reunion, 1985 : 7
Abbott-Kingwell Reunion, 2005 : 8
Abbott-Kingwell Reunion, 2010 : vii, 12, 67, 120, 147
Abbott/Shackleton Farm, North Dorchester Township, Ontario : 101
Abbott/Shackleton House, North Dorchester Township, Ontario : 74, 75, 76
Abbotts Cottage : 38, 39, 40
Abbotts Row : 39
Aitchison, Doug : 101
Aitchison, Heather : 101
Aitchison, Jacqueline : 101
Aitchison, Lois see Lois Shackleton
Ammerman, Susan (Susan Ketchapaw) : 121
Ammerman, Thomas : 121
Anderson, Debbie (Debbie Shackleton) : 109
Andrada, Josie : 12
Andrew, Vera (Vera Johnson) : 116
Andrews, Iain : 102
Anger, Harry : 99
Anger, Sylvia Beatrice (Sylvia Abbott) : 99
Arbroath District, Manitoba : 110
Arbroath School : 112
Archer, Lillie : 76
Armstrong, Elise Mary Lapthorne Abbott see Elise Abbott
Armstrong, Gordon Wray : 129
Armstrong, Howard : 129
Armstrong, Jack Rowse : 129
Armstrong, Murray : 129
Armstrong, William : 129
Arrand, Madeline (Madeline Pettit) : 116
Assisted Immigration Register : 60, 61
Avon Community Centre : 6, 7
Avon River, Devon : 13
Avon, Ontario : 1, 7
Aylmer, Ontario : 101, 109, 110, 111, 116, 118
Baker, Albert : 88
Bald, Evelyn (Evelyn Abbott) : 89
Baldwin Family : 121
Baldwin, Abigail Ketchapaw see Abigail Ketchapaw
Baldwin, Agnes Mary (Agnes Kennedy) : 121, 122, 123
Baldwin, Anna Bandura see Anna Bandura
Baldwin, Beverley Lucille : 123
Baldwin, Calvin : 123
Baldwin, Charles Samuel : 121
Baldwin, Charles Stanley (Charlie) : vii, xiv, 7, 9, 12, 80, 123, 124
Baldwin, Cheryl Louise : 123
Baldwin, Clarence (Clare) Warren : 121, 122, 123, 124
Baldwin, Corbett : 123
Baldwin, Dale Victor : 123
Baldwin, Daniel Morgan : 123
Baldwin, Donald William : 123
Baldwin, Donna Marie Franklin see Donna Franklin
Baldwin, Florence Corbett see Florence Corbett
Baldwin, Iva Merle Williams see Iva Williams
Baldwin, Ivan Lee : 123
Baldwin, Jeffrey Wayne : 123
Baldwin, John Charles : 123
Baldwin, June Eunice (Eunice Tuck) : 12, 123
Baldwin, Lucille Small see Lucille Small
Baldwin, Marlene Longworth see Marlene Longworth
Baldwin, Melvin : 123
Baldwin, Nina Faye (Nina Ferris) : 123
Baldwin, Priscilla Rowse Abbott see Priscilla Rowse Abbott
Baldwin, Rebecca (Faye) Wilson see Rebecca (Faye) Wilson
Baldwin, Robert : 124
Baldwin, Ronald Clarence : 124
Baldwin, Ronald Samuel : 123

Baldwin, Samuel : 96, 119
Baldwin, Sarah Jane : 123
Baldwin, Sena Ann (Sena Abbott) : xii, 7, 96, 98, 99, 100, 119
Baldwin, Shirley Cornell see Shirley Cornell
Baldwin, Stephanie (Stephanie Gosnell) : 12, 123
Baldwin, Timothy Lyndon : 123
Baldwin, Victor Donald : 123
Baldwin, Warren : 119, 122, 124
Baldwin, Warren Brent : 123
Baldwin, Wayne Maurice : 123
Baldwin, William Llewellyn (Bill) : 123
Baldwin, William Vernon (Verne) : 121, 122, 123
Balkwell, Bonnie (Bonnie McGlynn) : 12, 124
Balkwell, Brian : 124
Balkwell, Lila Bernice Baldwin Jackson see Lila Baldwin
Balkwell, Max : 124
Balkwell, Robert : 124
Balkwell, Wendy : 124
Bandura, Anna (Anna Baldwin) : 123
Barons, Edward : 44
Bayham Township, Elgin County, Ontario : 121
Bayham United Church : 121
Belfast, Ireland : 110
Belmont Public and Continuation School : 116
Belmont, Ontario : 56, 63, 64, 69, 87, 90, 92, 101, 103, 119, 130, 135, 138
Belmont, Ontario, Economic conditions : 64
Berry, Thomas : 76
Bethel Cemetery : 99, 113
Biddex, Ann : 23
Biddulph Township, Ontario : 85
Blacksmiths : 11, 14, 15, 25, 27, 29, 30, 40, 56, 64, 71, 86, 130, 131, 144, 146
Bowles, Donald : xiv, 8, 111
Bowles, Fred : 111
Bowles, Garry : 111
Bowles, Vera Henry see Vera Henry
Brady, Marlyn Abbott Cross see Marlyn Abbott
Brady, William Milburn (Bill) : 12, 142
Brain, Brenda Reading see Brenda Reading

Brain, Chris : 12
Brain, Howard : xiv, 12, 94
Brain, Janice : xiv, 12
Brain, Kelly : 12
Brain, Larry Clifford : 94
Brain, Lee : 94
Bratt, Mary Ann Cooper see Mary Ann Cooper
Bratt, Mary Jane (Mary Jane Abbott) : 90, 92, 93
Bratt, Samuel Oakley : 90
Brooks, Sarah Jane (Sarah Woolley) : 109
Brower, Donald : 101
Brower, Linda Shackleton see Linda Shackleton
Brower, Mary Ann : 101
Brower, Ron : 101
Brown, Calvin : 105
Brown, Connie (Connie Parsons) : 109
Brown, David : 12
Brown, Dennis : 7, 105
Brown, Emily : 12
Brown, Ethyn : 12
Brown, Judy Shackleton see Judy Shackleton
Brown, Kayd : 12
Brown, Neil : 7, 105
Brown, Randy : 7, 105
Brown, Sarah Jane : 12
Brown, Sheila : 7, 105
Buckfastleigh, Devon : 17
Buckfastleigh, William Abbott of (1614-) : 17
Budden, Byron : 109
Budden, Robert : 109
Budden, Tracey : 109
Buist, Andrew : 103
Buist, Christopher : 103
Buist, Mary Evelyn Shackleton see Mary Evelyn Shackleton
Buist, Terry : 103
Burgess, Charlene : 104
Burgess, Darryl : 104
Burgess, Diane Shackleton see Diane Shackleton
Burgess, Leslee : 104
Burgess, Wayne : 104

Burrell, William : 73
Byron, Ontario : 138
Cadleigh Farm : 44, 45, 46, 48, 54
Cadleigh House : 48
Cadleigh Manor : 45, 46, 47, 48, 50, 51
Cadleigh Manor Bed and Breakfast : 46, 49
Cadleigh, Devon : 46
Campbell, Laura Woolley Shackleton see Laura Woolley
Catfish Creek, Ontario : 109
Cave, Catherine : 12
Cave, Estelle : 7
Cemeteries see Dorchester Union Cemetery; Eden Cemetery; Grandview Memorial Cemetery; Haynecourt Military Cemetery; Oakland Cemetery
Chambers, Rosalene (Rosalene Garton) : 103
Cheese Factory : 127, 128
Cider : 30, 36, 39, 40
Clandeboye, Ontario : 130
Clark, Bernice (Bernice Duffin) : 12, 143
Cline, Edna (Edna Jackson) : 103
Clinton Township, Michigan : 128
Coleman, Philip : 16
Cooke, Adelaide : 104
Cooke, Colin : 104
Cooper, Mary Ann (Mary Ann Bratt) : 90
Corbett, Florence (Florence Baldwin) : 123
Cornell, Shirley (Shirley Baldwin) : 123
Coulthard, Karen (Karen Shackleton) : 101
County Tyrone, Northern Ireland : 135
Crawford, Joyce Shackleton see Joyce Shackleton
Crawford, Krista : 104
Crawford, Ross : 104
Crawford, Scott : 104
Credit Valley Railway : 64
Cross, Bradley Raymond : 142
Cross, Brenda Norine : 142
Cross, Raymond (Ray) James : 7, 142
Culp, Jean : 102
Dale, Brenda Shackleton see Brenda Shackleton
Dale, Dave : 105

Dale, Gregory : 105
Dale, Robert : 105
Dale, Steven : 105
Dance, Betty (Diane) : 101
Dance, Betty Shackleton see Betty Shackleton
Dance, Charles : 101
Dance, David : 101
Dance, Marcia : 101
Dance, Raymond : 101
Dart River, Devon : 13
Dartmoor : 13, 46
Dartnell, Ellen Adeline (Ellen Reading) Horning : 94
Davis, Danny : 8
Davis, Robin Scammell see Robin Scammell
Dawson, Lorraine (Lorraine Shackleton) : 101
DeCaire, Georgette (Georgette Dunn) : 129
Deacon, Catherine : 130
Deacon, Sarah (Sarah Abbott) : 85, 130, 131
Deacon, William : 130
Dean Prior Parish, Devon : 20
Dean Prior, Devon : 17, 20
Dean, Krista : 109
Dean, Rebecca : 109
Dean, Scott : 109
Dean, Sharon Shackleton see Sharon Shackleton
Dean, William Ross : 109
Deketele, Ralph : 102
Delaware Township, Ontario : 104
Delf, Marjorie (Marjorie Henry) : 111
Demaray, Elda (Elda Abbott) : 128
Demaray, Teresa (Teresa Abbott) : 128
Dennis, John : 70
Dennis, Myrtle : 121
Derewlany, Andy : 101
Derewlany, Dana : 101
Derewlany, Darrin : 101
Derewlany, Wanda Shackleton see Wanda Shackleton
Derkson, Brent : 112
Derkson, Dale : 112
Derkson, Joyce Harland see Joyce Harland

Derkson, Kimberley : 112
Derkson, Ronald William : 112
Derkson, Roxanne : 112
Derkson, Shaunalee : 12, 112
Detroit, Michigan : 123, 129
Devon, Economic conditions : 20, 56
Devon, England : xii, 13, 144
Donovan, Claudia Reading see Claudia Reading
Donovan, John Fredrick Stokes : 94
Donovan, Patrick : 94
Donovan, Paul : 94
Dorchester Union Cemetery : 66, 67, 80, 88, 92, 108, 118, 129, 134, 138, 143
Dorchester, Ontario : 2, 61, 63, 80, 128, 131, 146
Drager, Jacquelin Elizabeth (Jacquelin Abbott) : 142
Drowning, Accidental : 128
Duffin, Bernice Clark see Bernice Clark
Duffin, Bob : 12
Duffin, Elmer William : 143
Duffin, Joseph (Joe) William : 143
Duffin, Kimberley Ann : 143
Duffin, Mark Robert : 143
Duffin, Mary (Jean) Abbott see Mary (Jean) Abbott
Duffin, Robert (Bob) William : 143
Dunbar, Jean (Jean Houghton) : xiv, 7, 12, 108
Dunn Farm : 101
Dunn, Carl : 129
Dunn, Cheryl : 129
Dunn, Geoffrey : 129
Dunn, Georgette DeCaire see Georgette DeCaire
Dunn, Larry : 129
Dunn, Margaret Abbott see Margaret Abbott
Eaton Family : 114
Eaton, Harriet (Harriet Abbott) : 3, 114, 115, 118
Eaton, James (1844-) : 114
Eaton, Mary Ann Moore see Mary Ann Moore
Eden Cemetery : 123, 124
Eden, Ontario : 96, 119, 123
Ekfrid Township, Ontario : 85
Elgin County, Ontario : 63, 103, 110

Emigration : 56, 125
English, Beatrice (Beatrice Vennard) : 110
Erme River, Devon : 13, 16
Ermington Parish, Devon : 14, 15, 16, 56, 96
Ermington, Devon : 16, 17, 20, 43, 50, 54, 56, 86, 119, 130
Essay, Jackie (Jackie Parsons) : 109
Estate of Christopher Lethbridge (1760-1827) : 42
Estate of George (Lorne) Shackleton : 107, 108
Estate of Philip Abbott (1801-1874) : 40
Estate of William Abbott (1832-1914) : 78, 79, 80, 146, 147
Evans, Charlotte : 68
Evans, James : 68
Evans, John (1805-1885) : 68
Evans, John (1844-) : 68
Evans, Martha : 68
Evans, Mary Victoria (Mary Victoria Abbott) : 68, 74, 80, 81, 139, 146
Evans, Sarah (1839-1877) : 68
Evans, Sarah Robinson : 68
Evans, Thomas : 68
Eveland, Maxine : 12
Farm life : 105
Ferguson, Catherine Mary : 102
Ferguson, Clara (Clara Pettit) : 116
Ferguson, Corinne Ginou see Corinne Ginou
Ferguson, Dean Colin : 102
Ferguson, Douglas Colin : 102
Ferguson, Gail : 8, 12, 102, 134
Ferguson, Gordon : 102, 103
Ferguson, Hazel May Shackleton see Hazel May Shackleton
Ferguson, Kent Douglas : 102
Ferguson, Kirsten Suzanne : 102
Ferguson, Margaret Ellen (Margaret Abbott) : 143
Ferguson, Mary Starr see Mary Starr
Ferguson, Robert (Bob) Gordon : 102
Ferguson, Robert (Geordon) : 102
Ferguson, Rose Mary Wecsey see Mary Wecsey
Ferris, Arnold : 123
Ferris, Karen Ann : 123
Ferris, Nina Faye Baldwin see Nina Baldwin

First Annual Abbott Picnic, 1911 : 2, 147
Fishback, Beatrice (Beatrice Talbot) Brinklow : 89
Fletcher, Brenda : 12
Fletcher, Launie : 12
Fletcher, Scott : 12
Fortey, Brian John : 142
Fortey, Joyce Abbott see Joyce Abbott
Fortey, June Elizabeth : 142
Fortey, Karen Norine : 142
Fortey, Kelly Ann : 142
Fortey, Kenneth (Wayne) : 142
Fortey, Kenneth John : 142
Fox, Elsie (Elsie Abbott) : 88
Franklin, Donna Marie (Donna Baldwin) : 123
Franklin, Heather : 12
Franklin, Shirley Moody see Shirley Moody
Galt, Ontario : 93
Gardiner, Bridget : 25
Garton Family : 103
Garton, Amy : 103
Garton, Carolyn : 103
Garton, Donald : 103
Garton, Dorothy Ilene Shackleton see Dorothy Ilene Shackleton
Garton, Dorothy Marlene (Marlene Travis) : 7, 103
Garton, Elmer : 103
Garton, Gary : 103
Garton, Glen : 103
Garton, James : 103
Garton, Karen : 103
Garton, Larry : 103
Garton, Margaret (Margaret Pogue) : 103
Garton, Mary Schreurs see Mary Schreurs
Garton, Rosalene Chambers see Rosalene Chambers
Garton, Scott : 103
Gates, Edna (Edna Kennedy) : 123
Gee, Gladys : 139, 140
Gee, Kathleen Elnora (Kay Abbott) : 143
Gibb, Charles (Andy) : 101
Gibb, Cynthia : 101
Gibb, Elaine Shackleton see Francis (Elaine) Shackleton

Gibb, Marjorie (Gail) : 101
Gibb, Nancy : 101
Gibb, Ron : 101
Gibbon's Park : 6, 8
Gibbon's Park : 7
Gilbert, Norma : 101
Gill, Gary : 12, 105
Ginou, Corinne (Corey Ferguson) : 102
Gladstone General Store : 101, 106, 107, 128, 129
Gladstone School : 4, 71, 104
Gladstone, Ontario : 64, 70, 71, 106, 107, 114, 119, 127, 128, 129, 138
Glanworth, Ontario : 8, 63, 86, 87, 88
Glencoe, Ontario : 142
Glencolin, Malahide Township, Ontario : 101
Glencolin, Manitoba : 99
Godwell House, Ugborough, Ivybridge, Devon : 42
Gosnell, Alannah : 12
Gosnell, Andrew : 12
Gosnell, Stephanie Baldwin see Stephanie Baldwin
Gosnell, Tom : 12
Graham, Elizabeth (Elizabeth Vennard) : 110
Grand Trunk Railway : 61, 62
Grandview Memorial Cemetery : 89
Great Western Railway : 61
Great Western Railway Station : 61, 62
Greer, Elizabeth (Elizabeth McCord) : 135
Grose, Stella (Stella Shackleton) : 101
Guy Lombardo : 88
Haileybury, Ontario : 94
Hamilton, Ontario : 61, 94
Hamlyn, Eleanor (Eleanor Rowse) : 22, 24, 25
Hamlyn, John : 25
Hammond, Ronee (Ronee Shackleton) : 109
Harland, Brad : 8, 112
Harland, Brian : 112
Harland, Campbell : 112
Harland, Delmer : 112
Harland, Harvey : 8
Harland, John : 112

Index   163

Harland, Joyce : xiv, 8, 12
Harland, Joyce (Joyce Derkson) : 112, 113
Harland, Juli : 112
Harland, Lorinda (Lorinda Maruca) : 8, 112
Harland, Lulu Loretta Abbott see Lulu Loretta Abbott
Harland, Melvin : 99, 112, 113
Harland, Melvin (Wayne) : 8, 12, 112
Harland, Nicholas : 112
Harland, Paul : 112
Harland, Robert : 8
Harland, Robert (Harvey) : 112
Harland, Sharon Paulishyn see Sharon Paulishyn
Harland, Tamara : 112
Harland, Velma Lee see Velma Lee
Harold Abbott & Sons : 142
Harrietsville Women's Institute : 105
Harrietsville, Ontario : 1, 68, 70, 72, 96, 114
Hawley, Blanche (Blanche Shackleton) : 7, 104
Haynecourt Military Cemetery : 133
Henderson, Ann (Ann Shackleton) : 101
Henry, Alma Coral Abbott see Alma Coral Abbott
Henry, Barbara : 8, 111
Henry, Bob : 111
Henry, Clarence : 111
Henry, Connie Woodward see Connie Woodward
Henry, Dennis : 111
Henry, Douglas : 111
Henry, Joanne : 8, 111
Henry, Linda : 111
Henry, Marjorie Delf see Marjorie Delf
Henry, Robert : 111
Henry, Roberta : 8, 111
Henry, Ruby (Ruby Scammell) : 8, 111
Henry, Steven : 111
Henry, Terry : 111
Henry, Vera (Vera Bowles) : 8, 111
Herschel, Saskatchewan : 11
Hewbank, Harry : 104
Hewbank, Karyn : 104
Hewbank, Kimberly : 104

Hewbank, Nancy : 104
Hewbank, Ruth Shackleton see Ruth Shackleton
Hewbank, Timothy : 104
Hext, Elinor (Elinor Hamlyn) : 25
Highland Memory Gardens, Toronto, Ontario : 103
Hodgins, Margaret Elise (Elsie Abbott) : 138
Holdon, Gladys Rose (Gladys Abbott) : 138
Home Children : 73, 121
Honiton-on-Otter, Devon : 17
Horton, Harriet : 125
Horton, Harriet Hamlyn (Harriet Abbott) : 38, 39, 40
Horton, William : 38
Hortop, Mary Anne (Mary Parker) : 86
Hough, Myrna Parsons see Myrna Parsons
Houghton, Bruce : 108
Houghton, Carol : 108
Houghton, David : 108
Houghton, Diane : 7, 12
Houghton, Donna : 108
Houghton, Edna (Edna Martindale) : 108
Houghton, Ellen Alzina Abbott see Ellen Alzina Abbott
Houghton, Ethel (Marion) (Marion Sypher) : 108
Houghton, Glen : 108
Houghton, Glenn : 108
Houghton, Harold see Harold Young
Houghton, James : 108
Houghton, Jean Dunbar see Jean Dunbar
Houghton, Jimmy : 7
Houghton, Leah Ketchabaw see Leah Ketchabaw
Houghton, Lee : 108
Houghton, Marion Sneddon see Marion Sneddon
Houghton, Mary : 108
Houghton, Richard : 108
Houghton, Ronald : 108
Houghton, Rosemary : 108
Houghton, Roy : 108
Houghton, Russell : 7, 108
Houghton, Sylvia (Sylvia Shackleton) : 6, 7, 103, 108
Houghton, Thomas : 108
Houghton, Vernon : 7, 12, 108

Houghton, William : 108
Houghton, William (Ewart) : 108
Houghton, William Ewart (Earl) : 108
Howard, Margaret (Margaret Reading) : 94
Hubbard, Albert : 114
Hudson, Kim (Kim Shackleton) : 109
Hunt, Ellison : 12
Hunt, Eula Abbott see Eula Abbott
Hunt, George : 128
Hunt, Jim : 128
Hunt, Judith : 128
Hunt, Lewis : 7, 128
Hunter, Dorothy (Dorothy Shackleton) : 109
Immigration to Canada, 1871 : 82
Ingersoll, Ontario : 99, 103, 128, 129
Innes, Norine (Norine Abbott) : 7, 142, 143
Innkeepers : 27, 29, 40, 130
Ion, Alyce-Jean Salmon see Alyce Salmon
Ion, Jayne : 94
Ion, Russell : 94
Ion, Russell Thomas : 94
Ivybridge, Devon : 25, 41, 90
Jackson, Dennis : 103
Jackson, Edna Cline see Edna Cline
Jackson, Grace (Grace Shackleton) : 101
Jackson, Lila Bernice (Lila Balkwell) Baldwin : 124
Jackson, Louise (Louise Shackleton) : 12, 103
Jackson, Stanley (Bus) : 124
Johnson Family : 116
Johnson, Alberta Christina (Allie) Abbott see Alberta (Allie) Abbott
Johnson, Edna (Edna Winnington-Ingram) : 116
Johnson, Elva Erie (Elva Pilkington) : 116
Johnson, Elva Lydia Abbott see Elva Lydia Abbott
Johnson, Emerson : 116
Johnson, Emma Myrtle Abbott see Emma Abbott
Johnson, Ezra : 116
Johnson, Grace : 12
Johnson, Grace Morris see Grace Morris
Johnson, Irene : 12

Johnson, James : 116
Johnson, Jane : 116
Johnson, John : 116
Johnson, John Edwin (Johnny) : 116
Johnson, Mary Whitesides see Mary Whitesides
Johnson, Murray : 116
Johnson, Ralph : 12, 116
Johnson, Robert : 116
Johnson, Vera Andrew see Vera Andrew
Kennedy, Agnes Mary Baldwin see Agnes Baldwin
Kennedy, Brian Allan : 123
Kennedy, Charles Arnold : 123
Kennedy, Charles Lee : 123
Kennedy, Charles Madison : 123
Kennedy, Clinton Kenneth : 123
Kennedy, Dianne Louise : 123
Kennedy, Edna Gates see Edna Gates
Kennedy, Erie Beatrice (Erie Stewart) : 123
Kennedy, Gary Harley : 123
Kennedy, Harley Russell : 123
Kennedy, Hazel Rennie see Hazel Rennie
Kennedy, Joyce Arlene : 123
Kennedy, Lois Jean : 123
Kennedy, Marilyn Agnes : 123
Kennedy, Mary Alene : 123
Kennedy, Nellie Geraldine : 123
Kennedy, Ruby Dell (Ruby Moody) : xii, 7, 123
Kennedy, Sandra Ann : 123
Kennedy, Walter Lee : 123
Kennedy, Wayne Robert : 123
Ketchabaw, Leah (Leah Houghton) : 108
Ketchapaw, Abigail (Abigail Baldwin) : 96, 119, 121
Ketchapaw, Jacob : 121
Ketchapaw, Susan Ammerman see Susan Ammerman
Kidd, Kristi : 8
Kidd, Tessa : 8
Kingsteignton, Devon : 38
Kingwell Family : 107
Kingwell, Annie : 108
Kingwell, Bernard : xii, 6, 7, 12, 38

Index 165

Kingwell, Charles : 119
Kingwell, Ellen : 38
Kingwell, Emmaline : 38
Kingwell, Frances : 38
Kingwell, Isaac : 11, 38, 77
Kingwell, James : 38
Kingwell, Jim : 108
Kingwell, Kelly : 7
Kingwell, Miriam : 38
Kingwell, Nellie : 119
Kingwell, Nigel : 7, 12
Kingwell, Philip : 6, 11, 38, 60, 77
Kingwell, Prudence : 7
Kingwell, Sean : 12
Kingwell, William : 6, 38
Knott Family : 108
Knott, Ethel : 101
Lake Ontario : 61
Lamb, Ethel (Ethel Shackleton) : 105
Land Ownership : 56, 57, 144, 146
Lapthorne Family : 125
Lapthorne, Annie (Annie Abbott) : 3, 4, 84, 114, 125, 126, 127, 129
Lapthorne, Elizabeth : 60, 84, 125
Lapthorne, Frederick : 125
Lapthorne, John : 84, 125, 127
Lapthorne, Mary : 125, 127
Lapthorne, Mary (Mary Luxton) : 84
Lawson, Diane : 116
Lawson, Donna : 116
Lawson, Leta Pettit see Leta Pettit
Lawson, Mary Jean : 116
Lawson, Peter : 6, 116
Lee Mill Bridge, Devon : xii, 25, 28, 29, 30, 37, 38, 40, 53
Lee Mill Bridge, Devon, Map : 29, 30, 36, 37
Lee, Velma (Velma Harland) : 8, 112
Leonard, Mae : 66
Lethbridge tombstones, St. Peter and St. Paul Church Ermington, Devon : 52
Lethbridge, Albert : 40, 44

Lethbridge, Ann (Ann Rowse) : 84
Lethbridge, Christopher : 84
Lethbridge, Christopher (1760-1827) : 42
Lethbridge, Christopher (1802-1865) : 84
Lethbridge, Elizabeth (Elizabeth Barons) : 40, 44
Lethbridge, Frederic (1835-6) : 40
Lethbridge, Garland (1830-1899) : 84
Lethbridge, George : 85
Lethbridge, James : 85
Lethbridge, John : 85
Lethbridge, Laura : 40, 44, 54
Lethbridge, Lydia (Lydia Abbott) : 6, 13, 15, 20, 25, 40, 41, 43, 44, 53, 54, 55, 58, 64, 65, 66, 67, 84, 85, 119, 127, 146
Lethbridge, Mary : 85
Lethbridge, Sarah Windeatt (1821-) : 43
Lethbridge, Sophia (1843-4) : 40
Lethbridge, Thomas : 85
Lethbridge, Thomas (1796-1861) : 20, 25, 40, 42, 43, 44, 45, 50, 84, 130
Lethbridge, Thomas (1839-) : 44
Lethbridge, Thomas (1839-1909) : 40
Lethbridge, William : 85
Lindsay, Ontario : 89
Liverpool, England : 58
Locke, Susan : 12
Lockwood, Margaret (Marg Abbott) : 6, 12
Lockwood, Mary (Marg Abbott) : 142
London Hunt Club Grounds : 2
London Township : 125
London Township, Ontario : 86, 130
London, Ontario : 61, 63, 84, 85, 88, 102, 124, 125, 128, 129, 131, 134, 138, 139
Longfield Family : 107
Longworth, Marlene (Marlene Baldwin) : 7, 12, 123
Lonnee, Chantelle : 94
Lonnee, Clare (Shultzee) Reading see Clare (Shultzee) Reading
Lonnee, Claudine : 94
Lonnee, John James : 94
Lonnee, Mark : 94
Lonnee, Matthew : 94

Love, Eva : 104
Love, Irma Louise Shackleton see Irma Louise Shackleton
Love, John (Jack) : 104
Love, Loralee (Loralee Aarts) : 104
Love, Peter : 104
Lovell's Directory of 1882 : 71
Lovell's Business and Professional Directory of Ontario, 1882 : 72, 92
Lucan, Ontario : 130
Lyneham, Devon : 90
Macdonald District, South Norfolk Municipality, Manitoba : 99
Maddock, Priscilla (Priscilla Turpin) : 22
Malahide Township, Ontario : 98, 103
Malpass Family : 102
Malpass, Alma Laura Shackleton see Alma Laura Shackleton
Malpass, Jean Culp see Jean Culp
Malpass, Lynn : 102
Malpass, Murray : 102
Malpass, Nancy (Nancy Murchison) : 102
Malpass, Todd : 102
Malpass, William (Bill) : 102
Manitoba : xii, 7, 99
Map of Devonshire see Devon, Map
Maple Grove and beyond… to Eden (Memoir) : 124
Maple Grove, Ontario : 123, 124
Marriage Oath of John Rowse Turpin (1779-1841) and Eleanor (Eleanor Rowse) Hamlyn : 24
Marriage Oath of Roger Abbott and Miriam Metherel : 19
Marriage Registration of John Turpin Rowse (1747-1821) and Ann (Ann Rowse) Turpin : 23
Martin, Mary Jane (Mary Jane Shackleton) : 109
Martindale, Ansel : 108
Martindale, Betty Jean : 108
Martindale, Daniel : 108
Martindale, Dorothy : 108
Martindale, Edna Houghton see Edna Houghton
Martindale, Pat : 108
Martindale, Robert : 108
Martindale, Shirley : 108
Martindale, Thomas : 108

Maruca, Darren : 8
Maruca, Lorinda Harland see Lorinda Harland
Maruca, Sydney : 8
Matchetville District, Manitoba : 112
Matchetville United Church Women's Club : 113
Matthews, Grace (Grace Rowse) : 23
Maxwell, John (Max) Abbott : 139
McCord, Elizabeth Greer see Elizabeth Greer
McCord, Joseph : 135
McCord, Sara (Sara Abbott) : 3, 71, 135, 136, 137
McCracken, Betty : 12
McCracken, Evelyn Talbot see Evelyn Talbot
McCracken, James Lambert : 89
McCracken, Jim : 6
McCracken, Rick : 12, 89
McCracken, Sally (Sally Crawford) : 89
McDonald, Bob : 101
McDonald, Joan : 101
McDonald, Marie Shackleton see Marie Shackleton
McDonald, Robert (Dean) : 101
McDonald, Roberta Henry see Roberta Henry
McDonald, Rodney : 101
McDonald, Stan : 8
McGlynn, Bonnie Balkwell see Bonnie Balkwell
McGlynn, Doug : 12
McIntyre, Bertha (Shackleton) : 109
McKee, Florence (Florence Shackleton) : 104
Medland, Johanna (Joanna Metherel) : 20, 43
Medland, Sapience (Sapience Lethbridge) : 42
Melbourne, Ontario : 89, 129
Metherel Family : 50
Metherel, Elizabeth (Elizabeth Lethbridge) : 20, 40, 43, 44, 50
Metherel, John : 20
Metherel, John (1765-1830) : 20, 43
Metherel, Miriam (Miriam Abbott) : 17, 18, 20
Metherel, William (1795-) : 40
Metolli, Juliana (Juliana Romain) : 103
Michigan State Penitentiary : 95
Middlesex County, Ontario : vii, 56, 63, 139
Millin, Susanna (Susanna Lethbridge) : 42

Minneapolis, Minnesota : 94
Moffat, Muriel (Muriel Talbot) : 89
Mohr, William : 92
Moody, Gerald : 123
Moody, Blake : 123
Moody, Dwight : 123
Moody, Gordon : 123
Moody, Ruby Kennedy see Ruby Kennedy
Moody, Shirley (Shirley Franklin) : 12, 120, 123
Moon, Andrew : 94
Moon, Joyce (Joy) Salmon see Joy Salmon
Moore, Mary Ann (Mary Ann Eaton) : 114
Morris, Grace (Grace Johnson) : 116
Mosa, Township : 130
Mosseley, Ontario : 128
Mount Brydges, Ontario : 89
Mrs (Sena) Abbott's Book : 99
Mumford, Richard : 28
Murchison, David : 102
Murchison, Joan : 102
Murchison, Morris : 102
Murchison, Nancy Malpass see Nancy Malpass
Nagdown (Ship) : 18
Newfoundland : 18
Newfoundland fishing trade : 20
Newman, Hazel (Hazel Young) : 108
Newton Abbot, Devon : 20
Niagara-on-the-Lake, Ontario : 89
Nicholls, Sarah : 40
Norrington, Ryan : 7
North Bay, Ontario : 128
North Dorchester Heritage Book Committee : xiv
North Dorchester Township, Ontario : vii, 25, 56, 64, 69, 70, 71, 84, 85, 86, 96, 101, 102, 127, 135, 139, 146
O'Neill, William : 130
Oakland Cemetery : 138
Odanski, Ron : 104
Odanski, Trevor : 104
Oil Springs, Ontario : 89
Ontario Agricultural College, Guelph : 103, 104

Ontario, Economic conditions : 56, 57
Orchards : 28, 30, 33, 36, 40
Orwell, Ontario : 96
Owen Sound, Ontario : 110
O'Neill, Mary Ann : 130
O'Reilly, Anne : xiv
Paris, Ontario : 6
Parker, Alexander Edward : 86
Parker, Mary (Mary Abbott) : 3
Parker, Mary Anne Hortop see Mary Anne Hortop
Parker, Mary Page (Mary Abbott) : 86, 87, 88
Parsons, Christopher : 109
Parsons, Connie : 12
Parsons, Connie Brown see Connie Brown
Parsons, Darby : 109
Parsons, Ernest : 109
Parsons, Jackie Essay see Jackie Essay
Parsons, Jeff : 109
Parsons, Jesse : 109
Parsons, Lena : 109
Parsons, Leon : 12, 109
Parsons, Leonard : 12, 109
Parsons, Marie Richardson see Marie Richardson
Parsons, Melissa : 109
Parsons, Michael : 109
Parsons, Myrna (Myrna Hough) : xiv, 12
Parsons, Myrna (Myrna Hough) Budden : 109
Parsons, Richard : 109
Parsons, Vera Shackleton see Vera Shackleton
Parsons, Verna (Verna Stratton) : xiv, 12, 109
Parsons, Walter : 12, 109
Parsons, Wayne : 109
Paulishyn, Sharon (Sharon Harland) : 8, 112
Pearse, Jane (Jane Abbott) : 17
Pennsylvania : 68
Petersen, Erna (Erna Vennard) : 110
Pettit, Clara Ferguson see Clara Ferguson
Pettit, Gordon Ross : 116
Pettit, James : 116
Pettit, Leta (Leta Lawson) : xiv, 2, 6, 12, 116, 118

Pettit, Madeline Arrand see Madeline Arrand
Pettit, Mary Ann (Maud) Abbott see Mary Ann (Maud) Abbott
Pettit, Melvin James : 116
Pettit, Murray : 116
Pettit, Ralph : 116
Pettit, Ronald : 116
Philip, Abbott, Albert (1895-1966) : 40
Phillips, Mary (Mary Abbott) : 17
Pilbey, Mary : 136
Pilkington, Carol : 116
Pilkington, Donna : 116
Pilkington, Elva Erie Johnson see Elva Erie Johnson
Pilkington, Fred : 116
Pilkington, Jerry : 116
Pilkington, William : 116
Pinafore Park : 6, 8
Plym River, Devon : 13
Plymouth, Devon : 13, 54, 86
Plympton St. Mary : 15
Plympton St. Mary Parish, Devon : 6, 23, 28, 29, 38
Pneumonia (Cause of Death) : 92
Pogue, Darryl : 103
Pogue, Denise : 103
Pogue, Donna : 103
Pogue, Margaret Garton see Margaret Garton
Pogue, Ray : 103
Port Stanley, Ontario : 3, 128
Port Talbot, Ontario : 108
Pottersburg, Ontario : 88
Prairie Bible Institute : 94
Pressey Family : 107
Pretty, Constance (Connie) : 101
Priddle, Agatha Ryder see Agatha Ryder
Priddle, Barbara : 94
Priddle, Diane : 94
Priddle, Elizabeth : 94
Priddle, George : 94
Priddle, Lillian Blanche Abbott see Lillian Blanche Abbott
Priddle, Nancy : 94
Priddle, Susan : 94

Priddle, William Welmore : 94
Putman, Raymond : 101
Putnam, Cheryl : 101
Putnam, Marylyne : 101
Putnam, Robert : 101
Putnam, Valerie : 101
Putnam, William : 101
Pyatt, Anne (Anne Abbott) : 128
Quebec City, Quebec : 58, 61
Raleigh Township, Kent County : 84
Reading, Ada Clare Abbott see Ada Abbott
Reading, Brenda (Brenda Brain) : 12, 94
Reading, Charles (Douglas) : 94
Reading, Clare (Clare Lonnee) : 94
Reading, Clare (Shultzee Lonee) : 12
Reading, Claudia (Claudia Donovan) : 94
Reading, Dorothy Clare (Dorothy Salmon) : 94
Reading, Ellen Adeline Horning Dartnell see Ellen Horning
Reading, John Charles : 94
Reading, Margaret Howard see Margaret Howard
Reading, Marjorie Eileen : 94
Reeve (elected official) : 101
Rennie, Hazel (Hazel Kennedy) : 123
Reunions see Abbott-Kingwell Reunion; First Annual Abbott Picnic, 1911; Third Annual Abbott Picnic, 1913; Abbott-Kingwell Reunion, 1922; Abbott-Kingwell Reunion, 1940; Abbott-Kingwell Reunion, 1948; Abbott-Kingwell Reunion, 1985; Abbott-Kingwell Reunion, 2005; Abbott-Kingwell Reunion, 2010.
Richardson, Marie (Marie Parsons) : 109
Richardson, Ruth (Ruth Abbott) : 8, 142
Rickard, Elizabeth (Elizabeth Abbott) : 75, 76, 139, 140, 143
Rickard, Elizabeth Sadler see Elizabeth Sadler
Rickard, Philip Hendy : 139
Ridgetown Agricultural College : 142
Rigsby, Alex : 105
Rigsby, Hawley : 105
Rigsby, Janet Shackleton see Janet Shackleton
Rigsby, Jim : 105
Rock, Brenda : 8

Rock, Sheryl : 8
Rolston, Oliver : 76
Romain, Archer Aleksander : 103
Romain, Breeze Susannah (Breeze Romain Rose) : 102
Romain, Joseph : xv, 8, 102
Romain, Juliana Metolli see Juliana Metolli
Romain, Lionel Joseph : 103
Romain, Simone Rose : 103
Rommel, Renee : 104
Rose, Callum Joseph : 103
Rose, Ewan : 103
Rossendale Cemetery : 110, 111
Rossendale, Manitoba : 110
Row, Earl : 3
Row, Mary (Mary Shackleton) : 3
Row, Mary Shackleton see Mary Shackleton
Rowe, John : 28
Rowse, Ann (1786-) : 23
Rowse, Ann (1809-) : 25
Rowse, Edwin : 127
Rowse, Eleanor (1804-) : 25
Rowse, Eliza Hamblyn (1816-) : 25
Rowse, Elizabeth : 40
Rowse, Grace (1789-) : 23
Rowse, James Hele (1790-) : 23
Rowse, James Hele (1800-) : 25
Rowse, John Hamblyn (1802-) : 25
Rowse, John Lethbridge : 25, 84, 127
Rowse, John Turpin (1747-1821) : 22, 23
Rowse, Joseph Henry (1810-) : 25
Rowse, Mary : 23
Rowse, Mary (1782-) : 23
Rowse, Mary (1807-) : 25
Rowse, Mary Ann (1817-) : 25
Rowse, Priscilla (1784-) : 23
Rowse, Priscilla (Priscilla Abbott) : 17, 22, 25, 29, 40, 77, 84, 125
Rowse, Richard (1814-) : 25
Rowse, Sarah : 22, 23
Rowse, William (1812-) : 25
Ryder, Agatha (Agatha Priddle) : 94

S.S. Prussian (Steamship) : 58, 59
S.S. Sardinian (Steamship) : 135
Sadler, Elizabeth (Elizabeth Rickard) : 139
Sales, Beatrice : 139, 140
Salmon, Alan : 94
Salmon, Alyce-Jean (Alyce Ion) : 94
Salmon, Barton : 94
Salmon, Dorothy Clare Reading see Dorothy Reading
Salmon, Joyce (Joy Moon) : 94
Salt cod : 18, 20
Sampson, James : 23
Sandover, Ellen : 38
Sandover, William : 38, 40
Sapper : 131
Sarnia, Ontario : 89
Saskatchewan : 6
Scammell, Barry : 111
Scammell, Bert : 111
Scammell, Delmer : 111
Scammell, Jean : 111
Scammell, Jim : 8, 111
Scammell, John : 111
Scammell, Robin (Robin Davis) : 8, 111
Scammell, Ruby Henry see Ruby Henry
Scammell, Sandra : 111
Schreurs, Mary (Mary Garton) : 103
Schuel, Douglas : 89
Schuel, Joanne : 89
Schuel, Robert : 89
Schuel, Robert J. : 89
Seccombe, Joan Jenney (Joan Lethbridge) : 42
Shackelton see Shackleton
Shackleton Auction Barn : 6
Shackleton Family Reunion : 1
Shackleton, Allan : 103
Shackleton, Alma Laura (Alma Malpass) : 75, 101, 102, 106
Shackleton, Arnold (Verne) : 7, 101, 104, 106
Shackleton, Bertha McIntyre see Bertha McIntyre
Shackleton, Betty Diane (Betty Dance) : 101
Shackleton, Bill : 12

Shackleton, Blanche Hawley see Blanche Hawley
Shackleton, Bonnie : 101
Shackleton, Brenda (Brenda Dale) : 105
Shackleton, Brent : 12, 101
Shackleton, Brian : 101, 109
Shackleton, Bruce : 105
Shackleton, Cameron : 109
Shackleton, Carmen : 109
Shackleton, Carol (Carol Shiels) : 101
Shackleton, Carol Williams see Carol Williams
Shackleton, Caylee : 109
Shackleton, Christine : 12, 104
Shackleton, Christopher : 105
Shackleton, Clayton Robert : 3, 75, 101, 103, 106, 107
Shackleton, Clayton Roy : 103
Shackleton, Clifford : 101
Shackleton, Connie Pretty see Constance (Connie) Pretty
Shackleton, Dan : 101
Shackleton, Darren : 109
Shackleton, David : 102, 103
Shackleton, Debbie Anderson see Debbie Anderson
Shackleton, Deborah : 103
Shackleton, Debra : 101
Shackleton, Dennis : 101
Shackleton, Derek : 102
Shackleton, Destiny : 7, 12, 103
Shackleton, Diane (Diane Burgess) : 12
Shackleton, Donald (Larry) : 103
Shackleton, Donald Ross : 3, 75, 101, 103, 106
Shackleton, Donna Jean (Jean Putnam) : 101
Shackleton, Dorothy Hunter see Dorothy Hunter
Shackleton, Dorothy Ilene (Dorothy Garton) : 3, 4, 7, 12, 75, 99, 101, 103, 106
Shackleton, Douglas : 109
Shackleton, Edna Lorraine (Lorraine Tuff) : 103
Shackleton, Erin : 105
Shackleton, Ethel Knott see Ethel Knott
Shackleton, Ethel Lamb see Ethel Lamb
Shackleton, Florence McKee see Florence McKee
Shackleton, Frances (Elaine) (Elaine Gibb) : 101

Shackleton, Gary : 109
Shackleton, George (Lorne) : 2, 3, 75, 101, 106, 109, 139
Shackleton, Gerald : 101
Shackleton, Glen Brian : 101
Shackleton, Glenna (Jane) : 101
Shackleton, Gord : 101
Shackleton, Grace (Marie) (Marie McDonald) : 101
Shackleton, Grace Jackson see Grace Jackson
Shackleton, Gwendolyn (Gwendolyn Tracey) : 109
Shackleton, Harry Orville : 75, 101, 104, 106
Shackleton, Hazel May (Hazel Ferguson) : 1, 3, 7, 8, 12, 75, 101, 102, 103, 106
Shackleton, Hilary : 104
Shackleton, Ian : 101
Shackleton, Irma Louise (Irma Love) : 101, 104, 106, 107
Shackleton, Jackson (Wayne) : xiv, 1, 101
Shackleton, Jane : 105
Shackleton, Janet (Janet Rigsby) : xiv, 7, 105
Shackleton, Jason : 109
Shackleton, Jay : 109
Shackleton, Jeffrey : 103, 109
Shackleton, Jessica (Jessica Wilson) : 109
Shackleton, Joan : 101
Shackleton, Joanna : 104
Shackleton, John : 109
Shackleton, John Robert : 3, 109
Shackleton, Joyce (Joyce Crawford) : 103
Shackleton, Judy : 101
Shackleton, Judy (Judy Brown) : 7, 12, 105
Shackleton, Julie : 109
Shackleton, Karen : 101
Shackleton, Karen Coulthard see Karen Coulthard
Shackleton, Kathryn : 101
Shackleton, Ken : 12
Shackleton, Kenneth : 109
Shackleton, Kevin : xiv, 29, 104, 134
Shackleton, Kim Hudson see Kim Hudson
Shackleton, Laura : 105
Shackleton, Laura (Laura Strickler) : 109
Shackleton, Leone Silverthorn see Leone Silverthorn

Shackleton, Leslie (Les) : 6, 8, 12, 109
Shackleton, Linda (Linda Brower) : 101
Shackleton, Linda Sobon see Linda Sobon
Shackleton, Lisa : 104
Shackleton, Lisa Underhill see Lisa Underhill
Shackleton, Lois Jane (Lois Aitchison) : 101
Shackleton, Lorraine Dawson see Lorraine Dawson
Shackleton, Louise Jackson see Louise Jackson
Shackleton, Mallory-Lynne : 109
Shackleton, Margaret : 12, 104
Shackleton, Margaret May (Maggie) Abbott see Margaret May (Maggie) Abbott
Shackleton, Marilyn (Marilyn Walker) : 103
Shackleton, Mark : 109
Shackleton, Mary (Mary Row) : 3
Shackleton, Mary Diane (Diane Burgess) : 103
Shackleton, Mary Evelyn (Mary Evelyn Buist) : 103
Shackleton, Mary Jane Martin see Mary Jane Martin
Shackleton, Maurice Raymond : 101, 106
Shackleton, Mauricia : 105
Shackleton, Michael : 101, 109
Shackleton, Norma : 12
Shackleton, Norman : 105
Shackleton, Patricia (Pat Willis) : 103
Shackleton, Paul : 7, 105
Shackleton, Penny : 101
Shackleton, Robert : 101
Shackleton, Robert Lorne : 6, 7, 103, 104
Shackleton, Ron : 103
Shackleton, Ruby Abigail Abbott see Ruby Abigail Abbott
Shackleton, Ruth (Ruth Hewbank) : 103
Shackleton, Scott : 102
Shackleton, Sharon (Sharon Dean) : 109
Shackleton, Sharon Wintermute see Sharon Wintermute
Shackleton, Stella Grose see Stella Grose
Shackleton, Stewart : 3, 101
Shackleton, Stewart James (Jim) : 101
Shackleton, Stewart Lorne : 3, 101, 106
Shackleton, Susan : 101, 109
Shackleton, Terence : 103

Shackleton, Thomas : 105
Shackleton, Vera (Vera Parsons) : xiv, 109
Shackleton, Wanda (Wanda Derewlany) : 101
Shackleton, Wendy : 109
Shackleton, Whitney : 109
Shackleton, William (Bill) : 101
Shackleton, Wilma Willows see Wilma Willows
Shiels, Barbara : 101
Shiels, Brenda : 101
Shiels, Carol Shackleton see Carol Shackleton
Shiels, Randy : 101
Shiels, Robert (Jim) : 101
Ship's Passenger List : 60
Shultz, George : 130
Silverthorn, Leone (Leone Shackleton) : 109
Small, Lucille (Lucille Baldwin) : 123
Smith, Gavin : 12
Smiths Arms Inn : 29, 30, 36, 39, 40
Smiths Arms Inn see also Westward Inn
Smiths Cottages : 40
Sneddon, Marion (Marion Houghton) : 108
Sobon, Linda (Linda Shackleton) : 104
South Brent, Devon : 25
South Dorchester Township, Ontario : 101, 109
South Norfolk, Manitoba : 110
South Park Cemetery : 108
Southgate/O'Neill Cemetery : 130
Southwest England, Economic conditions 1860-1880 : 56
Springbank Park, London, Ontario : 4, 6
Springfield Cemetery : 108
Springfield Kinsey Cemetery : 109
Springfield, Ontario : 1, 6
St. George's Churchyard, Modbury Devon : 43
St. Lawrence River : 61
St. Paul's Anglican Cathedral, London : 102
St. Peter and St. Paul Church Burial Ground, Ermington, Devon : 50
St. Peter and St. Paul Church, Ermington, Devon : 50, 52, 54
St. Thomas, Ontario : 64, 89, 108, 128, 142
Starr, Mary Elizabeth (Mary Ferguson) : 102

Stevens, Neil : 114
Stewart, Calvin : 123
Stewart, Beverly : 123
Stewart, Daniel : 12, 67, 123
Stewart, David : 123
Stewart, Erie Beatrice Kennedy see Erie Kennedy
Stewart, James : 123
Stewart, Reginald : 123
Stewartstown, Northern Ireland : 135
Stratford, Ontario : 101
Stratton, Barry : 109
Stratton, Danny : 109
Stratton, Trevor : 109
Stratton, Verna Parsons see Verna Parsons
Strickler, John : 109
Strickler, Laura Shackleton see Laura Shackleton
Strong Family : 96
Sutherland, Helena A. : 119
Sweetman, Brian : 12
Sweetman, Susan : 12
Swift Current, Saskatchewan : 80, 146
Sypher, Bob : 109
Sypher, Colleen : 109
Sypher, Ethel (Marion) Houghton see Ethel (Marion) Houghton
Sypher, Frank : 109
Sypher, Frederick : 109
Sypher, Michael : 109
Sypher, Russell : 109
Sypher, Sylvia : 109
Talbot, Beatrice Brinkow Fishback see Beatrice Brinkow
Talbot, Bill : 89
Talbot, Denny : 89
Talbot, Evelyn (Evelyn McCracken) : 6, 89
Talbot, Glenda : 89
Talbot, Harold : 89
Talbot, Jeffrey : 89
Talbot, Jim : 89
Talbot, Mary Jane : 89
Talbot, Mary Pearl Abbott see Mary Pearl Abbott
Talbot, Muriel Moffat see Muriel Moffat

Talbot, Ruby : 89
Talbot, Wendy : 89
Talbot, William (1865-1941) : 89
Talbot, William (1925-2013) : 89
Tapsall Family : 107
Taylor, Margaret (Margaret Abbott) : 99
Thamesford, Ontario : 128, 131
Third Annual Abbott Picnic, 1913 : 2
Thorndale Community Centre : 8
Thorndale, Ontario : 1, 12, 87, 142
Tillsonburg, Ontario : 96
Tithe Apportionment Map : 29
Tithe Apportionments : 28, 43
Tombstone of William and Mary Abbott : 80
Tombstones : 50, 66
Toronto Emigrant Office : 61
Toronto Public Library : 102
Toronto, Ontario : 61, 62, 102, 143
Tracey, Ashley : 109
Tracey, Gwen Shackleton see Gwendolyn Shackleton
Tracey, Mark : 109
Tracey, Robert : 109
Tracey, Tyler : 109
Traher, Edwin : 38
Travis, Bradley : 7, 103
Travis, Brian : 103
Travis, Marlene Garton see Dorothy (Marlene) Garton
Travis, Sean : 7, 103
Treherne Area History Committee : xii
Treherne Railway Station : 113
Treherne, Manitoba : 8, 99, 111
Tuck, Blair : 123
Tuck, June (Eunice) Baldwin see June (Eunice) Baldwin
Tuck, Roger : 12, 123
Tuck, Susan : 123
Tuff, David : 104
Tuff, Lorraine Shackleton Odanski see Edna (Lorraine) Shackleton
Turpin Family : 50
Turpin, Ann (Ann Rowse) : 22, 23

Turpin, John (1719-1786) : 22
Turpin, John Rowse (1779-1841) : 22, 23, 24, 25
Typhoid Fever : 130
Ugborough, Devon : 54
Underhill, Lisa : 104
VanKoughnett, Loreen Abbott see Loreen Abbott
VanKoughnett, Roy : 128
Veal, Grace (Grace Abbott) : 17
Vennard, Alexander : 110
Vennard, Beatrice English see Beatrice English
Vennard, David : 110
Vennard, Donald : 110
Vennard, Donna : 110
Vennard, Doris : 110
Vennard, Elizabeth Graham see Elizabeth Graham
Vennard, Elsie (Elsie Wilke) : 110
Vennard, Erna Petersen see Erna Peterson
Vennard, Grace Agnes Mary Abbott see Grace Agnes Mary Abbott
Vennard, John : 110
Vennard, Matthew : 110
Vennard, Norman : 110
Vennard, Patrick : 110
Vennard, Raymond : 110
Vennard, Wendy : 110
Vennard, William : 110
Venning Family : 84
Victualer see Innkeepers
Voters List for 1935 : 138
Voters List for 1968 : 138
Wages, Various Trades : 83
Walker, Doug : 103
Walker, Marilyn Shackleton see Marilyn Shackleton
Walker, Mark : 103
Walls Family : 108
Ward, John : 43
Water Wheel Cottage : 40
Wayne, Michigan : 7
Wecsey, Rose Mary (Mary Ferguson) : 102
Wesleyan Methodism : 56
West Nissouri Township, Ontario : 88, 139, 143

West, Mary : 25
Western Abbott Reunion : 7, 112
Western Ontario Regiment : 123, 131, 133
Westlake, Devon : 15, 16
Westminster Township, Ontario : 88, 90, 92, 130
Westminster, Ontario : 63
Westward Inn : 30, 31, 33, 34, 35, 36
White, Yvonne (Yvonne Abbott) : 128
Whitesides, Mary (Mary Johnson) : 116
Wilke, Elaine : 8
Wilke, Elsie Vennard see Elsie Vennard
Wilke, John : 110
Wilke, Leonard (Len) : 110
Wilke, Linda : 110
Wilke, Reg : 8
Wilke, Reginald : 110
Wilke, Sheila : 110
Wilke, Wendell : 110
Williams, Carol (Carol Shackleton) : 103
Williams, Eliza : 43
Williams, Iva Merle (Iva Baldwin) : 123
Williams, Lee : 124
Williams, Richard : 43
Willis, Carolyn : 103
Willis, Garry : 103
Willis, Jaret : 103
Willis, John : 28
Willis, Patricia Shackleton see Pat Shackleton
Willis, Robin : 103
Willows, Wilma (Wilma Shackleton) : 103
Willsey, Freda Abbott see Freda Abbott
Willsey, Harvey : 128
Wilson, Bertrand : 89
Wilson, Erma Marilynn (Erma Schuel) : 88, 89
Wilson, Gladys Emma Abbott see Gladys Emma Abbott
Wilson, Glen Albert : 89
Wilson, Jeffrey : 109
Wilson, Jessica Shackleton see Jessica Shackleton
Wilson, Karalee : 109
Wilson, Lisa : 109

Wilson, Rebecca Faye (Faye Baldwin) : 123
Wilson, Wayne : 109
Windeatt, Sarah (Sarah Lethbridge) (1800-) : 43
Windsor, Ontario : 89, 102
Winnington-Ingram, Edna Johnson see Edna Johnson
Winnington-Ingram, Gerald : 116
Winnington-Ingram, Janet : 116
Winnington-Ingram, Judy : 116
Winnipeg, Manitoba : 8, 80, 99, 111, 146
Wintermute, Sharon (Sharon Shackleton) : 105
Witherton, Henry (1700-) : 20
Witherton, Joan (Joan Metherel) : 20
Wolsey, Tom : 103
Wonderland Gardens : 6
Woodland Farm : 40, 43, 54
Woodland Village, Devon : 43
Woodward, Connie (Connie Henry) : 8, 111
Woolley, George : 109
Woolley, Laura (Laura Shackleton Campbell) : 3, 101, 108
Woolley, Sarah Jane Brooks see Sarah Jane Brooks
World War (1914-1918) : 95, 123, 131, 134
World War (1939-1945) : 89, 110, 128
Yarmouth Township, Elgin County : 69
Yealm River, Devon : 13, 15, 30, 34, 36, 40
Yealmbridge, Devon : 14, 15, 39, 135
Yealmpton Parish, Devon : 14
Yealmpton, Devon : 15, 54, 84
Yeoman, Alfred Philip : 38
Yeoman, Blanche Abbott : 38
Yeoman, Francis Robert : 38
Yeoman, Robert : 38
Young Family : 108
Young, Douglas : 108
Young, Gloria : 108
Young, Harold (Houghton) : 108
Young, Hazel Newman see Hazel Newman
Young, Jack : 108
Young, Peter : 108
Young, Sharon : 108
Zahorodni, Jerry : 12

Index

CPSIA information can be obtained
at www.ICGtesting.com
Printed in the USA
LVHW070645241019
635154LV00013B/101/P